THE PLAN B CHRONICLES

Divorce. Defiance. Liberation.

MEREDITH BEARDMORE

Library Tales Publishing

Published by:
Library Tales Publishing
www.LibraryTalesPublishing.com
www.Facebook.com/LibraryTalesPublishing

Copyright © 2025 by Meredith Beardmore

No part of this publication may be reproduced, stored in a retrieval system, or transmitted in any form or by any means, electronic, mechanical, photocopying, recording, scanning, or otherwise, except as permitted under Sections 107 or 108 of the 1976 United States Copyright Act, without the prior written permission of the Publisher.

Requests to the Publisher for permission should be addressed to the Legal Department, Library Tales Publishing, P.O Box 20407, New York, NY, 10023. 1-800-754-5016; Legal@LibraryTales.com

Trademarks: Library Tales Publishing, Library Tales, the Library Tales Publishing logo, and related trade dress are trademarks or registered trademarks of Library Tales Publishing, Inc. and/or its affiliates in the United States and other countries, and may not be used without written permission. All other trademarks are the property of their respective owners.

For general information on our other products and services, please contact our Customer Care Department at 1-800-754-5016, or fax 917-463-0892. For technical support, please visit www.LibraryTalesPublishing.com

Library Tales Publishing also publishes its books in a variety of electronic formats. Every content that appears in print is available in electronic books.

** Printed in the United States of America **
9 7 9 8 8 9 4 4 1 0 2 3 4

"This book is dedicated to all the women who have had their hearts shattered and were left to gather the pieces alone. May it serve as a reminder of your indomitable fire."

A Note on Truth

This memoir is a reflection of my personal journey—an attempt to make sense of my experiences and share them meaningfully. To protect privacy, some names, identifying details, and events have been altered or fictionalized. Any resemblance to actual individuals, living or deceased, is purely coincidental.

I have done my best to recount the truth as I remember it, though memory is inherently subjective. This is my perspective—not an objective account. My intention is not to harm or misrepresent anyone, but to offer insight and connection to those who may find themselves in similar circumstances.

I hold deep respect for all who have been part of my story—those who have shaped me, whether for better or worse, and for the lessons that came with both. Even the most difficult chapters are shared with the hope of fostering growth—for myself and for anyone who might read these words.

Part I

"Even loss and betrayal can bring us awakening." ~ Buddha

7/23/22

ON MY KNEES

"Where the road bends abruptly, take short steps" ~ Ernest Bramah

As my mother and I scramble to pack up the car, I realize I have to move my (at-the-time) husband's car to get mine out since he had blocked it in during his arrest. I grab the spare keys from the kitchen and rush out the back door, eager to get started on the nine-hour drive to my parents' house in Ohio.

"You need to be gone tonight because there is a chance, a small chance, that he'll be released from jail tonight."

The statement from the cops keeps echoing in my head. I am still unable to believe what has transpired over the past five hours.

I quickly pry the car door open, using my hand under my t-shirt to keep from getting burned. The dashboard reads 101 degrees as I sink into the driver's seat. It takes me a second to turn the car on—I'm distracted by the thick, awful smell of weed and the tiny, empty Ketel One nips strewn across the passenger seat.

"That explains a lot," I whisper to myself as I hear the engine turn on. I crank the air conditioner to the highest level, hoping it will cool down the car and push the heat out, but it only worsens the stench. Holding my nose with one hand, I steer the car in reverse down the crooked driveway with the other. I park quickly, equally eager to breathe clean air and to get out of his trashed car.

I put my hand on the door handle but hesitate to open it. I feel glued to the car seat—not from the sweat dripping between my thighs, which I can see running down the seat—but from something else. An energetic stillness. Like something from another dimension is stopping me, insisting that I take in my surroundings. The trash on the passenger seat and floor. The alcohol bottles. Then my eyes meet a small, zipped-up black bag.

The same energy spins around my hand, as if something—or someone—is guiding me, placing it on the black bag. But no one is physically here. I can only describe it as supernatural, as if my hand already knows I need to see what's inside.

I open the bag and find a container full of weed and a crumpled-up receipt. Normally, I'd never look at a receipt. In fact, I don't find them necessary and always refuse one if given a choice. But this isn't like any other time. That strange energy still lingers around my hand. That "glued to the seat" feeling still holds me in place.

I slowly smooth the receipt on the console's surface, assuming I'll find purchases for gasoline and a 5-hour Energy drink. Instead, I see two charges: one for a 5-hour Energy drink, as I had assumed, and the other for a One-Step Plan B emergency contraception.

Confusion and sickness overtake my body. The energy around my hand vanishes, leaving me alone with racing thoughts. I keep rereading the receipt, unable to put two and two together at first. I had my fallopian tubes removed due to potential complications if I got pregnant again. Since my husband was afraid of anything medical, I took one for the team.

"No, this must be his friend's receipt," I say aloud, hoping that will make it true, hoping that will make sense.

"...But what friend?"

I rack my brain for a logical explanation for why this receipt is in my husband's bag. When the most logical (and obvious) explanation comes into my awareness, my body goes limp—legs like Jell-O, fingers like noodles.

I check the date. It's from the day before at 9:20 in the morning, somewhere in Brooklyn.

The urge to puke rises high in my throat, but since I haven't been able to eat due to the emotional stress of late, acidic bile bubbles up instead. I start to dissociate. Time stops, and I leave my body. I'm sitting in the passenger seat, unable to move, but I'm watching my face as if I'm in the front row of a movie theater, outside of myself.

I don't know how much time passes, but I eventually take a photo of the receipt, then try to stick it on the dashboard with a post-it I find on the floor. The intense New York heat makes its stickiness fail, so I have to search for another way to leave it. Instead, I shove it up into the tiny opening right above where you can read the speed limit, hoping he'll find it and know that I know.

I slowly walk up the driveway, sick from dizziness and betrayal, sometimes leaning against my condo's siding to keep my balance. I have to consciously watch each foot in front of me, willing them to move, one by one. Time continues to feel distorted, and the colors of my surroundings begin to vanish, muting and melding into a muddy gray. I can taste the sweat droplets forming on my lips as I open my mouth, forcing myself to breathe.

Just a few more steps to the back door.

"Move, Mere. You can do it. One more step," I encourage myself as the dizziness becomes overpowering.

Black spots cloud my vision as I will myself to breathe. To move. I know that soon I'll be with my mom, and I'll no longer be alone with this devastation.

Then everything goes black.

My mom later tells me that when she came out the back door, she found me bent over on all fours on the steaming-hot black concrete. I still wince thinking about how excruciating this must have been for her—seeing her daughter collapsed, facedown and unresponsive.

I can't speak. At some point, I finally manage to type in my phone's passcode, each number taking what feels like a minute to remember. My phone unlocks to the picture of the receipt on the screen. My mom grabs it, trying to understand what I'm showing her.

Then, boom. It clicks.

I don't remember our conversation. I just remember her wrapping her arms around my waist and picking me up off the ground. My knees are burned from pressing against the hot cement for so long.

I have no idea how I manage to drive the whole nine hours home to Ohio.

But I do.

7/28/22

HOLLOW

"Unlike other forms of psychological disorders, the core issue in trauma is reality" ~ Bessel van der Kolk

"Where am I?" I whisper to myself as I slowly come to consciousness.

Dappled sunlight filters through the leaves of the tree above me, swaying in the breeze, casting shifting patterns of shadow and light across my body. My head pounds, and I feel mulch poking into my scalp, twisting my hair. My surroundings gradually begin to sharpen. The weight of my skull feels too heavy to lift, and a sense of disorientation washes over me as I realize I'm lying on the ground in my parents' backyard.

How did I end up here? What happened to me?

Like shards of glass slowly piecing together into a shattered mirror, my memory begins to form. For days, I've been immersed in the labor of tending to my parents' garden, channeling my pain and grief into the meticulous care of their garden.

The sun's punishing rays only exacerbate the ache in my head and the gnawing emptiness in my stomach. My body feels frail and hollow. I hadn't realized just how much I had been neglecting myself—too consumed by my inner turmoil to heed the warning signs of exhaustion and dehydration. In my fervent pursuit of distraction, I've forgotten to tend to my own well-being.

I lie in the soil and slowly attempt to turn my head, focusing my gaze on the flowers I must have dropped when I lost consciousness. Radiant clusters of red verbena and white petunias fill my view, and for a split second, I feel calm. But my vision quickly blurs as pools of tears form, and it all comes flooding back in a rush of realization and regret.

Am I here? Am I real?

A wail emerges from my being, so fierce that it startles me. I feel the salt streams move down my cheeks as I shut my eyes and let out another guttural scream. With my eyes closed, I'm bombarded by quick flashes—like a disjointed movie trailer playing at full speed. Sirens. Police. The receipt.

I force my eyes open to make the trailer stop and focus again on the flowers.

"You're safe. Look at the flowers. They are safe," I whisper to myself.

I can't help but feel a pang of longing for the vibrant flowers that sit just out of my reach. These flower babies need to be cared for and watered. They are beautiful and strong. *I am weathered and weak.* I want to be one of them. I don't want to be human. I want simple. I want the pain to end.

I will myself to move my bones. I begin to crawl through the dirt, but the weight of grief and exhaustion presses down on me like a suffocating blanket. The movie trailer in my mind begins again, transporting me back to that steaming-hot concrete. It's as if my body has triggered the memory just by being in a similar physical position. It is etched in my memory, seared into my soul, like a brand. My physical helplessness is a visceral reminder of my reality.

No one is here to pick me up from the ground.

I cry out, "Mom!"

Then I remember—my parents took my son for the day to give me time alone.

I decide to focus on my breathing.

"Stop crying and focus. Keep your eyes open and breathe."

I obey.

A few movements forward, and I reach my water bottle, gulping down its contents until I hit the last drop. Next, I grab the crumpled sack of food from Wendy's that my mom left me, hoping I'd eat it. I snatch a handful of fries and stuff them into my mouth, chewing even though I can taste the soil from my fingers mixing with the salt.

I can barely push the food into my mouth. Nausea grips me, and I fear that anything entering my body will make me choke. My insides have been stuffed with falsehoods so tightly that the thought of adding anything more is unbearable. I feel my body housing all the lies, and I can't wash off the betrayals. I feel disgusting from the violation.

Discovering the Plan B confirmed that they didn't use protection —*at least once.*

Did I share my husband with his paramour on the same day?

I deserved to know before his penis entered me if it had been inside another person that day. If *he* had been inside another person that day.

A black, slimy substance fills up my stomach—left from him and her.

He was the one who cheated, so why do I feel like the dirty one?

"'No one will ever want you again."

There it is. The haunting self-hate that permeates my mind, leaving me feeling worthless.

I need to know if I have an STI.

What if I do?

How will I cope?

I'm scared. I'm scared. I'm scared.

I FORCE MORE dirty french fries into my mouth, and after some time, I feel my body reenergize, grateful for the calories. I have a moment of clarity. "I will die if I keep doing this to myself," I say out loud, and a wave of fear comes over me, followed by a deep knowing that if I stay on this path, I will die. I remind myself that I am okay and that I will know soon enough, but then I begin to fantasize about the relief that would be granted upon death. No more sadness, no more grief, no more nightmares, no more torment in my mind.

I truly understand passive suicidal ideation now. This is what all my clients were talking about. While I don't want to actually die, thinking about the fact that I have an option out of this pain provides a level of comfort and a sense of control. Life has been happening to me, without my permission, and my little family unit has been eviscerated. Nothing feels safe. I do not have any intent to harm myself, no plan for how I would do it, nor the means to make that happen. But if I could just not wake up, I wouldn't have to face it all. I could *avoid the pain.*

I sit with these passive suicidal thoughts and imagine the relief if I could just be unconscious for a few months until I can grasp my new reality. I try not to shame myself for these thoughts and instead step into my comfort zone by assessing my mental status. I begin to categorize my symptoms to determine my own diagnosis.

Suicidal thoughts? Check.
Flashbacks? Check.
Nightmares? Check.
Loss of appetite? Check.
Dissociation? Check.
Hypervigilance? Check.

Hmmm—sounds like PTSD with Depersonalization. "I can't be diagnosed with PTSD until I've had the symptoms for more than a month. Maybe it's an adjustment disorder, but this is more intense than that, so yeah, it's def PTSD," I whisper to myself. "How could I have PTSD? Did I fight in a war and see someone die? Did my house burn down? No. I'm a joke. Get a fucking grip!" my inner voice screams.

But come to think of it, my house did burn down. At least, that's how it feels. Everything I thought was real and true wasn't. Nothing is safe. The world doesn't feel safe. How could this happen?

"I am alone. I am alone. I am alone. I want to sleep. I just want to sleep."

I lay back down in the soil and focus again on the tree swaying in the wind above me. I remember doing this throughout my childhood; the trampoline was my safe haven, and I spent countless hours staring up at the leaves from my imaginary trampoline cocoon.

A wave of intense grief and compassion pours over me, thinking of that little girl. I cry for her and the future she dreamed of. I wish I could tell her that it gets better. But it doesn't.

8/6/22

RECEIPTS

"Each betrayal begins with trust" ~ *Martin Luther*

When I first come back to New York after the "incident," I meet up with my girlfriends and stay the night. We head out to dinner at a cozy little restaurant in Fort Greene to process everything. And even though it all feels surreal, I have a momentary sense of calm—and that, in and of itself, is a gift.

We indulge in cocktails and delicious food while recounting the details of the past three weeks. Twice, I notice people looking over at us, probably distracted by our loud laughter that quickly shifts into saddened cries, only to shift back again just as abruptly. I make several trips to the bathroom to wipe away my dripping mascara.

After the check is paid, we make our way to the corner for some fresh gelato as we venture back to Elara's apartment.

"Mere, you heard about Emrata, right?" Elara asks.

"Emrata" is short for Emily Ratajkowski. Most people know her as the stunning model who became famous after appearing in Robin Thicke's *Blurred Lines* music video, but we know her as the most exquisite writer.

Emily is arguably the most beautiful human on this planet while also being one of the most brilliant. I not only read her book, *My Body*, in paperback, but I also bought it on Audible so I could hear her narrate it after Elara told me that Emily cried while reading a particularly impactful part. She puts into words all the things that are often unsaid or difficult to articulate about women, their bodies, and how they are treated. It's obviously much more complex than that, and since I respect her so much and can't begin to do it justice, I urge you to just read it.

"No, what?" I ask.

"Oh shit, you don't know? She's getting a divorce. Her husband has been cheating on her."

"What? He cheated on *her*?" I shout, nearly slinging my empty cup of gelato in shock. "There's no way. No way. She's the most beautiful and brilliant creature on this Earth."

Our wise friend Leigh points out that cheating has nothing to do with a woman's appearance and everything to do with a man's insecurities.

"I never got good vibes from her husband when she mentioned him in her book. He had no idea what he had, and he didn't deserve her," I remark, as if I know their relationship intimately. He was protective of her at a party once, and that was the first time she had ever experienced that. To me, it felt like the bare minimum, and I'm sad she hadn't experienced better sooner.

THE INTERIOR of Elara's brownstone is magical at all hours, but nighttime is particularly special. From the drips of hardened candle wax on the gold candelabra to the ornate spiral staircase leading to the second floor, the place is a dream. Many months before Elara and her husband, James, obtained the brownstone, I had vivid dreams of it. I would call Elara up and tell her about her future space, excited by the possibilities it would hold.

See, Elara and James are special—an inspiring kind of couple, the best example of yin and yang. I knew their space had to reflect that magic, and of course, it does.

I'm comfy on the blow-up mattress set up in the first-floor living room, perfect for admiring the soaring ceilings, carved fireplaces, and special artwork curated by my dear friends, yet I can't sleep. It just feels strange not having my son cuddled up next to me since it has become a regular occurrence since the "incident."

Throughout the night, I keep waking from either nightmares or sudden bouts of diarrhea, probably the result of the excessive Mexican food and gin I consumed. Emily's situation keeps running through my mind. *I* could be cheated on, sure—but not Emily. It feels like such an injustice, and I wish I could tell her how amazing she is and that she doesn't deserve this.

Just when I start to drift off to sleep, my belly cramps and rumbles, followed by a sudden, intense urgency to get to the bathroom. My poor body is in shock from being fed—especially with spicy food and alcohol. "This is why I don't drink," I mutter to myself as I rush to the toilet.

With every trip to the bathroom, I Google the news about the Emrata cheating scandal in total disbelief. I just can't believe it. I keep compulsively reading articles from different news sites and scanning for Emily's likes on certain tweets, affirming that the accusations are true.

One reads, "Can't believe that little bitch cheated on Emily," and another, "Girls, how are we celebrating Emrata's divorce?" My favorite tweet that she liked was, "Emrata finally free from that man just proves that God is actually very real."

Yes. Thank you, God, for letting her know. And thank God I found that receipt.

8/12/22

DISBELIEF

"No amount of evidence will ever persuade an idiot" ~ Mark Twain

The first time the social worker from Child Protective Services comes over, I'm gripping my stomach, ready to puke. Technically speaking, I have nothing to be nervous about; I've already had a brief meeting with her via Zoom a few weeks prior to confirm our son is safe. I dismissed my initial bad feeling as superficially judgmental when she didn't know how to work Zoom—I even ended up sending her a link from my work account.

Regardless, Stacy comes in, and immediately I think, *She's not right*, though I don't have any specific reason to believe this. It's just an overwhelming sense. Then, she remarks that this will be quick since she has *much worse* cases. Ok...

As I recount that traumatic day, right when I'm starting to replay the violence, Stacy interrupts and asks for my mother to join us, casually remarking that she has a headache. My mom begins to speak, and when she briefly gets mixed up about dates, Stacy cuts in and says, "You guys are making me crazy!"

My mom and I are stunned. It's officially awkward.

I give Stacy a beat, allowing her space while her comment lingers in the air... but the silence drags on too long. It starts to feel like a weight, thickening the space between us. I can't stand it anymore.

Fine! I break the silence with the question I ultimately need to ask—the one that's gnawing at me.

"Stacy, have you seen Tripp?"

She doesn't hesitate, looking me in the eye and saying, "He told me that you two haven't been intimate in four to six months," as if that somehow justifies his affair.

Tears fill my eyes and splash my sunburned cheeks. I look away, shaking my head in disbelief. Not only am I not expecting this comment, but it also isn't true, and I have no idea why she is saying this.

"But he told me he always used protection," she says, trying to comfort me... as if that somehow made it okay.

"No, he didn't. Remember, I told you I found out about the cheating when I found the One Step Emergency Plan B receipt in his car?" I reply.

It doesn't click for her, so I spell it out clearly... with my mother standing there, giving me a slightly concerned, slightly cautious look. I think she fears how I will come across, knowing the pain I'm in and how strange Stacy is acting.

"She had to take the morning-after pill because they had sex without a condom, and she was not on birth control."

I swear, Stacy still doesn't get it. Her eyes don't widen, don't shift —it's as if the gravity of what I'm saying doesn't reach her. She stares at me blankly, as if I'm speaking a different language. When I mention that I'll be doing STD testing, she keeps saying, "You'd already know. You'd already see signs down there."

"WHAT?" I want to scream. "WHAT THE FUCK ARE YOU TALKING ABOUT, YOU FUCKING IDIOT?!"

But I don't. I nod as if to agree. It's clear he's already gotten to her. He's tall, charismatic, and (most importantly) manipulative. She's been duped, so let's just get this shit over with.

"I met with him, and he cried so much. I can tell he really loves you," she says, as if that's supposed to mean something.

Does this fucking woman think this is what I want—or need—to hear? This doesn't feel professional—this feels fucking *fucked up*.

The rest of the meeting is a blur. I can feel myself shutting down, detaching, watching the whole interaction like a movie—a terrible, disjointed, surreal movie, all from an outsider's view. It's dissociation, my body's way of protecting me.

Stacy goes on and on about all the cases she's handling and that she'll be back in a few weeks to get more information. After shutting the door and watching her happily walk down my front steps, I turn to my mom.

Neither of us speaks.

We just stare

Fall 2021

SOBER SEX

"Events do not just happen, but arrive by appointment." ~ *Epictetus*

During the fall of 2021, my marriage really began to feel, perhaps (*most definitely*), "strained." The main players in the breakdown were the pandemic, having a toddler, and sex—specifically, sober sex.

I desired to do it sober. I wasn't demanding it every time, but maybe just once in a while? And my reasoning probably isn't what you'd expect. I truly missed my husband's smell. That might sound strange, but it's science. Pheromones are chemical substances secreted outside the body—through sweat, urine, or even breast milk—that affect human attraction and reproduction. This explains why I always wanted to jump his bones after a workout. His sweat was never a turnoff because it intensified his particular... scent.

To me, his smell was a mixture of salt, campfire, and leather—and that was without any cologne.

Knowing this, you can understand my dismay when his scent went from delicious to nauseating. When those lovely pheromone chemicals were replaced by the awful stench of alcohol, I was angry. And jealous. That bottle of booze wasn't just stealing my husband's attention away from me—it was wrecking our sexual connection.

I expressed my desire for sober sex and how much the smell bothered me, but I was met with immense pushback. Like I was being too controlling and "no fun." And, after a while, I started to believe it. Maybe I *had* become those things to an extent.

The pandemic, like for many, had made me incredibly anxious, and being a new mom was not easy. I was navigating my new responsibilities, fully aware that I couldn't be as "free" as I had once been. I had a whole being to keep alive. I never wanted to stop being fun, especially not when it came to intimacy. But to be fair, we had never needed alcohol before when it came to sex, to connecting, to *having fun*—so why was it suddenly so important now?

We could go round and round in circles about it, and eventually, I'd just give up the fight. So, I came up with other ways to cope. I began avoiding kisses, which was sad, but I was trying to compromise. But then his alcohol consumption became a **daily** occurrence, and the alcohol would reek from his pores.

You know that smell. That foul, vinegar-like, toxic scent. And it really *is* toxic—the body is literally trying to release poison through sweat.

Next, I started switching positions during sex, acting like I *liked* my face pressed into a pillow the whole time. *Surprise, I didn't like it.* I actually wanted to make eye contact during our intimate time. But somehow, even then, the pillow wasn't blocking the smell enough. So, I started spraying it beforehand, inhaling fresh lavender as a momentary reprieve from the stench of whiskey. Eventually, even that stopped working.

I couldn't escape the smell seeping from his pores. I felt like I was suffocating—physically and emotionally.

When no amount of essential oils or fabric softener could mask it, I began asking if we could try another time… when he was sober.

This enraged him.

He would count out the long hours he worked on set, how hard he worked, and how he deserved to have sex with his wife.

Whenever he said those words, I'd feel foggy and disoriented, as if I'd suddenly been dropped into another marriage. The once *super liberal* man I married had morphed into a chauvinist, insisting that wives should always submit to their husband's needs.

"What are you talking about? I don't even know who you are right now!" I'd repeat, dumbfounded by who he'd become.

Please understand—we used to love describing ourselves as a *nontraditional* couple. We would talk shit about the stereotypes in heterosexual relationships, about how we could *never* have lived in the '50s.

This was a man who *loved* cleaning. He insisted on hand-washing dishes, even when we had a dishwasher. He took care of all the laundry and placed it, perfectly folded, in our drawers.

In the past, we rented out the third bedroom in our Astoria apartment on Airbnb. We were a great team—I handled the business side (scheduling, communication), and he handled the prepping (cleaning, bedding). Even after the Airbnb stint, we continued our lives seamlessly, focusing on our strengths. He appreciated my ability to handle the bills, and I appreciated his care for our home.

But as his addiction grew, his ability to carry out his responsibilities faded—then disappeared altogether.

I became even more "no fun"—but only because I had to pick up everything he left behind. My previous responsibilities, plus my husband's, plus a toddler.

AS IF ALL this wasn't enough, one night, my husband drunkenly stumbled into our little bathroom while I was doing the bedtime bath routine with our son. I was hit by the stench of alcohol as he opened the bathroom door. My first instinct was to pull my shirt up to cover my face, but I tried my best to keep my attention on our son and to not provoke a reaction out of him. As I leaned over the bathtub to finish helping my son, I was startled when the white shower suddenly swung in front of my face, blocking my view of our child. Without having time to turn my head, Tripp leaned behind me and, in a quiet voice, demanded, "Give me a blowjob."

"Are you fucking serious?" I whispered to him. "Our son is right there!"

"You're so boring. You don't know how to have fun anymore," he muttered.

I froze, stunned by his words. A chill ran through me, a creeping sense that he was a stranger. Fear settled in my chest—this was so different from how he had ever been with me. The fear made me back down. I began to apologize, promising to finish up with our son quickly, then give him all my attention.

"Too late. You killed the mood," he slurred at me as he left the room, slamming the door.

I sat in shock, unable to move for what felt like hours but was likely only a few seconds. I couldn't understand how I was always the problem. I kept replaying that last interaction in my head, searching for it to make sense, but it didn't.

My son made a big splash and smiled, unaware of what had just happened. I leaned over the tub to kiss his forehead, inhaling *his* familiar, comforting scent. I wondered why my husband didn't do the same. He used to be so present with us. I was beginning to feel like I had to choose between caring for my son or for my husband. And I knew in my bones that I'd choose my son every time.

The next day, my parents came into town. I was excited to take my mom upstate to an apple orchard with a pumpkin patch. It would be a fun day for our son, and there was even a chance we'd spot Martha Stewart, since it was rumored to be a favorite of hers.

After spending hours in the sun, chasing after our toddler, and failing to catch a glimpse of Martha, I returned home with a giant pretzel and dipping sauce from a gourmet vendor on site. I was so pumped to have childcare—I couldn't wait to snuggle in bed with my husband like old times, watching TV while enjoying a tasty treat.

I cheerfully entered the bedroom, eager to show him what I'd brought home, hoping this gesture would make up for our interaction from the night before. He shut his laptop immediately and said, "We need to have sex."

I laughed for a moment and joked, "Wow, how romantic."

He didn't move or smile.

"Oh come on, I was just teasing. Can I at least show you the delicious pretzel I got you first?" I asked with a smile.

He just stared. We had been together eight years at that point, and I couldn't read his expression. I approached the bed, still holding the stupid giant pretzel, when I was hit by a relentless wave of alcohol. The AC, blasting on high since it was unusually hot out, carried the stench straight into my nostrils. My nose instinctively crinkled.

Shit, I thought, *"He saw my nose move."* I immediately knew my facial reaction would upset him... and it did.

We argued for a few minutes, and then, out of nowhere, he smacked the pretzel out of my hand.

I stood there, stunned. Then, quietly, I knelt down to clean up the cheese sauce splattered everywhere. Without saying a word, he walked past me and shut the door behind him.

8/13/22

MR. GOOGLY EYES

"Tears are the silent language of grief" ~ Voltaire

HGTV, my mom's favorite channel, blares loudly in the exam room while I anxiously wait for my STD test to begin. Why is there even a TV in an exam room? I can't take the sound of it any longer, so I get up and shut it off. It feels good to have some control over my life. It's strange how the smallest things—things you *can* control—can bring such relief.

I lean my head back and close my eyes, further agitated by the crinkling sound of the medical paper lining my seat.

"Ugh, I can't stand the sound of this shit. Is this even necessary?" I mutter just as a young nurse enters with a smile.

"Okay, so what brings you in today?" she asks politely.

"I need STD testing," I reply, matter-of-factly.

"Were you exposed?"

Exposed. What a strange word in this moment. *No, he has been exposed for what he's done. I have been damaged... while being exposed to his bullshit.*

"Yes, I found out my husband has been cheating on me."

"Do you know how many people and for how long?"

I appreciate that she doesn't say, *I'm sorry*, before asking. I don't want sympathy. Maybe my body language tells her I'm not down for it. I just want to get the fucking test done and over with.

"I know of one. There could be more... I'm not sure. He had testing when he entered rehab, and he was negative for HIV, so I don't think I need that."

She nods in agreement and leaves to get the doctor.

In walks a thin, old, balding white man with thick glasses that make him look like he has "googly eyes" (thanks, Christopher Walken), much like the craft eyes I helped my son glue onto an art project the night before.

Ew. This gross old man is going to look at, and in, my vagina. Fuck. Fuck him, and fuck my ex.

I instinctively cross my legs tighter as he sits down. He explains that it can take 23 to 90 days after exposure for HIV to be detected—the time between infection and the production of antibodies—so he strongly encourages me to test for it. It requires blood work. I agree.

Then, he talks about recent research showing that women who swab themselves provide better results.

(*Of course* the results are better when women do it themselves. They don't feel uncomfortable having a stranger all up in their most intimate parts. Let alone *swabbing* them.)

Relief floods through me as I exhale. Dr. Googly Eyes isn't going to make me undress and get inspected.

In the bathroom, I insert the swabs just like I would a tampon, making sure to move them around in thorough circles, just as instructed. I pop them into their little cup, wash my over-it hands, and pass them off, grateful that the worst is over.

Next is blood work, and as odd as it sounds, I *want* to be stabbed. I want to see the blood leaving my body. It feels good to experience real pain—something that reflects how I feel inside. It makes me understand my clients who engage in NSSI (cutting, burning), how they do it to feel *physical* pain rather than emotional pain.

I guess I can thank Tripp for giving me deeper empathy for my clients.

Before Dr. Googly Eyes leaves, he tells me how to get my results and to contact him if I have any issues. Then, just as he steps into the doorway, he pauses.

"You deserve someone who respects you," he says. "I hope you find that."

I nod. And the moment the door shuts, I start to sob.

Hard.

I know I won't be able to stop.

So I pick up my things and continue crying—all the way out of the clinic. People watch and stare as I walk by.

I don't care.

I don't care, because it means so much that this doctor expressed care for me.

A man showed care for me.

8/15/22

UNSOLICITED ADVICE

"The less said the better" ~ Jane Austen

I eventually get my STD test results back, and it turns out I'm clean. However, time stops for no one, and I have to head back to Ohio for the two weeks between summer camp and Pre-K. I can't afford babysitters during that time and need my parents' help so I can continue running my private practice.

Before leaving, I have the locks changed and stop by the condo's management office next door to drop off the new keys and explain why they had to be changed in the first place.

I'd always been friendly with the receptionist, an Italian woman in her seventies. We'd often chat when I walked my dog—she'd spot me coming and, like clockwork, step outside to share her latest story or opinion. Some days, it was a welcome distraction; other days, I'd plan a different route if I wasn't in the mood to talk. She was one of those people who thought being a therapist meant you were always ready to listen. Still, I didn't mind her presence. She was harmless.

Or so I thought.

After giving her the watered-down version of the drug addiction and violent outbursts that led to the order of protection, expect to be met with understanding eyes and supportive words, validating my need for a divorce. Instead, I'm met with something entirely different.

"How could you divorce him so quickly? You're taking away his last thread of hope, his incentive to get better. Did you really need to file so fast?"

I'm stunned. I start listing more reasons, grasping for something that will make her see my side, but she just keeps going—about the importance of keeping a family together, about giving him a chance. And suddenly, I start to feel really bad about myself.

Am *I* the one breaking up the family? Could I fix this?

My son and I weren't enough to get him better before—why would now be any different?

Am I one of *those* women who isolates a child from their other parent? No. No, I *can't* do that.

Maybe I *am* making a mistake!

I leave the management office with the wind entirely absent from any hope of a sail. And then, back to Ohio I go.

I SPEND the entire first weekend back nearly despondent, unable to do more than play with my son or plant flowers for maybe half an hour before I inevitably need to lie down and just *stare*. I stare at the ceiling and wonder how it all went wrong. I replay every moment leading up to the "incident" and question who I am, especially now that this has happened to me.

I must be a terrible person. A terrible wife. A terrible mother.

How could I divorce him—*abandon* him—when he isn't well? But I *still* feel completely used up by him. I'm miserable.

How can *I* be responsible for breaking up the family? Aren't *his* actions what actually tore it apart?

I don't want to keep Jude from him. But I also don't want to put Jude in danger if he isn't sober.

...How did this happen?

This receptionist is unhappily married. I know because she told me—told me about how, the day she came home from the hospital after knee replacement surgery, her husband expected her to make him dinner. Most people would say she grew up in a time when you stayed together no matter what, that it was about dedication, love, or a moral compass. But I disagree.

Because, until 1964, an employer could refuse to hire a woman *simply because she was a woman.*

Until 1974, it was legal to refuse to sell a home to a woman *simply because she was a woman.*

Until 1988, refusing to rent to a woman with a child was *legal*.

Maybe my landlord couldn't leave because she *didn't have the option.*

Or maybe she resents me because I *do*.

I don't know.

After days of isolation and sadness in Ohio, I finally tell a friend all the things I've been stuck on—the mountain of noise I've been trying (and failing) to traverse. Said friend, in the truest sense of the word, replies and validates my thoughts with the following:

1. No one gets to guilt you about anything. You get to make your own decisions about what's right for *you*, for your *son*, and for your *future*.

2. You are *not* responsible for him. If his actions are so rooted in your relationship, then that means he's not doing anything to get better for the *right* reasons.

3. No one gets to *shame* you. He made his bed. And he can lie in it. There are so many people who think you're "supposed" to stay no matter what. That women are responsible for all the caregiving.

That we're supposed to tolerate *whatever garbage they present us with* for the sake of keeping things intact. That. Is. Bullshit. It's *trauma*. It's *unhealthy*. And research doesn't support it being in anyone's best interest. He's fucked himself so royally at this point. You are worthy of *more*, and *greater*, and *better*. Also. Fuck that receptionist! *(I'm irate on your behalf.)*

8/18/22

CAMERA ROLL

"The art of knowing is knowing what to ignore" ~ Rumi

I'm lying in my childhood bed, alone. My mom has already fallen asleep on the couch downstairs, her usual habit during any PBS show, while my son peacefully slumbers in my parents' bed. At the same time , I love and hate being in bed by myself. Becoming a single parent feels like I can never steal a moment just for me, but when I do, it is quiet and difficult; I have to actually hear the thoughts in my head.

The quiet of the house is interrupted only by the familiar sound of my dad's footsteps, signaling his own retreat to bed.

"Everyone is going to bed, so it's safe for me to do the same," I keep repeating to myself.

In an effort to drown out the voices in my head, I put on my headphones and set my Apple Music library to shuffle. At first, Christina Aguilera's fearless voice pulses in my ears, distracting me with her powerful vocals and sexual lyrics. Then, *Camera Roll* by Kacey Musgraves begins to play.

I had held off on listening to that album when it first came out, knowing it chronicled her journey through divorce. When it was released in October 2021, I was still holding out hope for a change in my marriage. Still, I purchased the album, knowing there was a chance I'd need her words eventually.

Now, I listen intently, realizing the title is quite literal—that only the happy moments are typically stored in your camera roll, imploring listeners to resist the temptation of scrolling through memory lane for its false, rose-tinted depiction of reality.

And yet, instead of heeding the song's very direct, very deliberate warning, I do the opposite.

I scroll way back in my camera roll, landing on a video of my husband. He is hiding behind our bedroom door, waiting for our six-month-old son to approach. Then, suddenly, he pops out, sending our son into shrieking fits of laughter as he runs to me.

I begin to sob uncontrollably. The video shamelessly, almost obnoxiously, confirms that he once loved us, that he once *wanted* to be a husband and a father. This was before the alcohol took over and dragged him down to the basement. It's like my soul remembers that it was once real—and my sorrow is actually justified.

I can't stop the tears. My breathing shifts from a normal cry to hyperventilation. I can't calm myself down, and I know I need a rest. But I also know I won't be able to will myself to sleep. I need Tylenol PM, or melatonin, or hell—even whiskey. Anything to bring me down.

My parents don't keep alcohol in the house, so that isn't an option. I scour the bathroom shelves, but I come up empty. I realize my dad would know where the Tylenol PM is. I'm torn between sneaking into his bedroom to search for it myself or waking him. My sobs are impossible to stifle, my tears clouding my vision, and he's my dad. So, in my vulnerability, I decide to wake him.

I put my hand on my dad's back. Through muffled sobs, I try to ask if I can have something to help me sleep. I expect him to mutter *yes* and roll over.

Instead, to my surprise, he is angry.

"I can barely understand you, and I was *just* about to fall asleep!" he says, his voice tight with frustration.

In shock, I walk out of the room and back to my bed. Granted, I'm sensitive to men—*even my dad*—especially when they raise their voices. But in this moment, when I am so raw and fragile, I can't take any kind of intensity.

A minute later, my dad comes into my room and starts opening a bottle of Tylenol PM as I begin to apologize.

"I'm so sorry, I was just watching and remembering this moment," I say, turning my phone toward him, hoping it will give him context for why I woke him.

He watches the video, and his face turns red.

"Here," he says as he opens the pill bottle. "Stop watching it. He's dead. *That guy is gone.* It's time to get over it."

He tosses the pills in my direction and walks out.

I sit there in silence.

I'm so confused. How did I make my dad *so* angry?

My mind immediately goes to my dad's childhood. He grew up in an environment where emotions were downplayed or dismissed. Navigating emotional situations has always been hard for him; anger is his default response.

My father has never liked tears or any heightened emotion from us—me, my sister, or my mother. He watched his own mother cry nonstop after my grandfather left her for the woman down the street, leaving her with six kids to raise. Whenever we cry, it's as if he's catapulted back in time, back to being a helpless child. And, growing up in the '60s and '70s, traditional gender roles made it so that anger was more acceptable—even desirable—for men. Crying threatens his sense of control, a direct challenge to decades of societal pressure to conform to a traditional masculine ideal.

And then I think about my parents' loss. My tears are making him *face* the pain he, too, is experiencing. He is losing a son-in-law, someone he thought would love and protect his daughter and grandson. He is grieving, too.

But here's the thing. At a certain age, we are no longer just victims of our past. We *must* work through our trauma so we don't pass it on.

Still, as his daughter, whether he intends to or not, I feel like a burden. I know my mother's time spent supporting me in New York after my ex's rehab stint took a toll on their marriage. They've been married for almost 48 years. Weeks apart is not their norm. They *rely* on each other. They *deserve* to be together.

I never imagined I'd be the obstacle keeping them apart.

I never want to *need* help.

And yet, here I am, reinforcing the negative belief I've developed over years of my husband's addiction and aggression toward me—*I am a nuisance.*

Then, my sadness shifts to anger.

Does he think I want to be here? That I want to be back in Ohio after my life blew up in my face? I've lost my husband, and my son lost his father—to drugs.

Everything inside me wants to lash out, to scream at my father. But I know better. It won't get me anywhere.

Hours later, deep into the night, I hear my mother washing dishes. It's something she has done my entire life—her sacred, quiet time when the house is still.

"Mom, I have to tell you something that happened a few hours ago," I say as she turns off the faucet. She wipes her wet hands on a dish towel and turns to me, concerned.

I explain everything. I go on and on about how messed up it was. She listens. And she agrees.

But then she says, "What good will it do to talk to him? He's not going to change. He doesn't know how to express himself. You just have to ignore him."

And I ultimately agree.

We know the routine. If we voice our feelings, he'll get quiet and withdrawn, and *we'll* be the ones who have to build him back up again. Restore homeostasis.

Wearily, I climb back into bed and pull the covers up to my neck. I stare out the window at the stars, wondering how it is that I'm experiencing the same feelings toward my father that I had after a fight with my husband.

I teeter between self-blame and intense guilt.

I am the problem.

My needs are too much for my husband. And for my dad. The pattern is undeniable—I am the common denominator.

Then, I think about my mother's detached response. How she instructed me to do the same.

My mother is thoughtful and loving. She isn't the problem.

And yet—she *knows* exactly what I'm feeling. She shares in it.

And I realize: *I've been conditioned to accept this behavior.*

To ignore. To overlook. To keep quiet.

But I don't want to be quiet anymore.

Part II

"I am out with lanterns, looking for myself." ~ Emily Dickinson

8/22/22

NOSE SWABBER

> *"How ridiculous and how strange to be surprised at anything which happens in life."* ~ Marcus Aurelius

*E*ver since discovering the Plan B receipt, I have scrutinized it *relentlessly*, analyzing every detail. I know the time, the day, and the location of purchase. With this information, I can pinpoint that my husband was likely texting the person who took the pill within the prior 24 hours.

Armed with facts and reasoning, I give my sister access to our phone records. She graciously color-codes them into *suspicious numbers* and *non-suspicious numbers,* and together, we zero in on the number connected to my husband's paramour. We can't pull up her name, but we know we're getting close.

After a few dud attempts at narrowing it down, I finally reach Macey—a super successful but very young second assistant director. Macey works behind the scenes of the same hit TV show alongside my husband and the *other woman.*

"Hi, I know this is really strange, and if you don't want to speak with me, I totally understand," I begin, my voice steady but urgent.

"But my husband has been cheating on me, and I suspect it's with someone on set. It might not be in my best interest to know who, but as you can imagine, this is all very shocking, and I just feel that I have a right to know."

Macey listens quietly on the other end.

"I have to say, I'm surprised to hear he cheated on you," she finally responds. "He always speaks so highly of you and constantly shares pictures of your son. I'm so sorry this happened to you. My mom went through the same thing with my dad growing up, so I'm painfully aware that people can live double lives."

I exhale with relief.

"I hope you can understand that I don't want to get too involved in this, but I do want to help you," she says after a pause. "I have the call sheet in front of me. What's the number?"

I recite it back to her without missing a beat—each number seared into my memory.

"Oh, that number *is* on the call sheet, but it isn't for the crew," she says. "It's for one of the health and safety workers. We had to hire an outside company to be on set to stay COVID-compliant. Her name is Lizzy Martin. I'm not super familiar with her, but she does the COVID screenings."

"She *does* the COVID screenings," I repeat, confused.

"Yeah, she does the nose swabbing."

"So, you're telling me I was cheated on with *the nose swabber*?"

Macey lets out a little laugh. "It appears so."

"What does she look like?" I blurt out, immediately realizing how pathetic I sound.

"I really don't know her, and if it's the person I'm thinking of, she's pretty young and kind of goth. It's strange—they aren't required to wear scrubs or anything," Macey explains.

"How young?" I demand.

"I mean, I'm considered young for my job, and I'm 25. We're probably around the same age if I had to guess, but I'm not 100% sure."

"Well, that's fucking disgusting," I reply sarcastically. Macey laughs in agreement.

"I have to go, but if you need anything, reach out. I'd like to keep this off the record. I won't mention anything to him, and I'd prefer you didn't say how you got this information," Macey requests.

"Of course. My lips are sealed, and I'm so grateful for your help. Seriously, it means so much."

"You're welcome. You'll survive this. I know, because my mother did, and she was the best mother *and* father ever," Macey emphasizes before ending the call.

I sit with tears in my eyes, my mind swirling in a tornado of new information. *Goth? Young? Nose swabber?*

Without hesitation, I log into our shared AT&T account and skim the phone records. There it is—the nose swabber's number, over and over again. Texts upon texts, then phone calls.

They're not even hiding it.

They think I don't know.

But I do.

There's a field next to each phone number where you can assign a name, and below it, a nickname.

I find her number.

Instead of entering "Lizzy Martin" as the name, I type "Replacement for my wife." Then, in the nickname box, I type "NOSE SWABBER." I click save and watch with grim satisfaction as the new labels populate the call log.

A sick sense of accomplishment washes over me. It's familiar. But this isn't a grad school test, and there's no reward for getting the right answer. Connecting the puzzle pieces won't fix anything. If anything, stitching it all together only highlights how shattered my life has become.

I press my forehead against the steering wheel, then bang it a few times before collapsing into my seat.

A guttural, animal-like howl erupts from deep within me.

How could he?

"UGGGHHHH," I moan out loud, startling myself awake. My hair is damp, my sheets are drenched—I've had another stress-nap nightmare. This time, it was Tripp and *her*.

I saw him undressing her, kissing her shoulders, making her giggle—just like he once did with me. She looked up at him with doll-like eyes, making him feel like a god with her submissive gestures and sexual adventurousness.

"Enough!" I scream, launching out of bed. I stomp around my room, searching for my laptop.

I need to see her.

I've resisted internet stalking, trying to be the *bigger person*. But fuck that. I *want* to know.

Tripp's sister confirmed it—the nose swabber is *the one*. The one who said she was *"helping him through a hard time."* The one who, when I finally mustered up the nerve to call, told me she was *"getting really tired"* and asked, "Can I call you tomorrow?" when I demanded to know if their relationship was romantic. The one who fucking *lied* to me.

I have her name, her phone number. I even know her voice.

But no trace of her online.

How does someone that young not have social media? No Facebook, no LinkedIn picture, no Instagram—nothing.

Then, a friend suggests checking *Venmo*.

And there she is.

She's supposedly 27, but she looks 17. Short bangs, silver-purple dyed hair, a black choker—I guess that's goth? She does have a cute smile.

I want to hate her.

I have visions of driving past her, launching an egg at her back, laughing maniacally as yolk splatters all over her dumb, punk-wannabe clothes. I want to call her and scream "WHORE!" before hanging up. I want her to *pay* for sleeping with my husband.

I want to shame her.

But why?

Why do I need to see her face *and* shame her?

On one hand, I want to match her face to the person in my nightmare—to put an image to this shit show. But if I'm being honest, I also want to compare myself to her. I want to zero in on her flaws, pick them apart, and find something—*anything*—that makes me feel even a little better.

Rationally, I know comparison is the thief of joy. It only diminishes my self-worth, wastes my time, and drains my energy. I know that obsessing over her will only get in the way of appreciating who *I* am—the things that make me unique, the stuff that makes me *loveable*.

But right now? I don't care about protecting myself.

I want to destroy.

As I stare at her picture, my insides turn to molten lava, and the once-boiling pain—numb from shock—erupts, coursing through my body like an earthquake. This is the first time I've ever felt rage that makes you physically *move*. My hands shake, then my arms, my head, my hips. The betrayal, the injustice, the disgust—it floods my being, demanding release. The despondency is gone. Now, I feel *everything*.

The lies. The sacrifices. The audacity.

Fuck him.

Fuck *her*.

I want to burn it all to the ground.

In a frenzy, I send her mother messages on Facebook, contorting myself for some kind of answer—since *she* won't respond to me. Almost instantly, my friends Leigh and Remy swoop in with the fastest *SOS don't-do-it* texts I've ever received.

"Doesn't serve you. Doesn't serve you. Doesn't serve you," Leigh writes.

"I don't care anymore," I shoot back.

"You're just tormenting yourself," she replies. "Knowing things about her is your way of seeking understanding. But realistically, the answers lie with Tripp. They lie in his addiction, *his* chaos, *his* selfishness. The answers lie in his inability to think of anyone but himself. In this instance, it literally could have been *anyone*. It just happened to be her."

"But I can't fucking take this," I text back, shaking. "He came in *her* while I was home caring for our son—the sweetest boy ever. What kind of fucking woman does that???"

"He was looking for someone to slap a Band-Aid on his self-loathing. A pause button to avoid accountability. He did what he did —not because of *her*—but because he is so self-absorbed he didn't give a shit about you. Which is why you were already proceeding with a divorce *before* you knew this. Having the information just adds insult to injury. It only confirms what your gut already knew."

I inhale sharply. "You're right."

I take a breath.

Then, Remy texts, worry laced through her words.

"I'm so conflicted because I don't want you to feel judged, but, Mere, I think you have to stop yourself from contacting her and her family. I just don't think it's the healthiest path for you. I'm also worried it could be used against you legally. If this escalates, she could claim harassment. I don't want anything making this harder for you. How can I help? Can you talk at 7:30?"

I groan. *Why are my friends so fucking levelheaded?*

But deep down, I know why I told them.

Because I *know* I'm not emotionally equipped to make the best decisions for myself right now.

Thankfully, Facebook allows users to unsend messages now.

I go back and delete everything. Immediately, I let my friends know.

"I love you. I'm not trying to be unsupportive at all," Remy replies. "I don't know how I would react in your place, and I honestly am *not* judging. I just didn't want anything to happen that could hurt you even more. Like her leaving a bad review for your business or something petty like that. You don't have to unsend it just because I mentioned that. You should do whatever *you* need for closure. I'm just so sorry for the rage. I wish you had gotten a chance to scream in his face."

Leigh chimes in, ever the psychologist. "We need to identify a replacement behavior for when you feel compelled to dig. This isn't about *her*. It's his mess. I know it's hard. You can't confront him and get the answers you want. You can't make him *feel* your rage in the raw way you need. But trust me—his consequences are coming. You don't have to deliver them."

"What serves *you* is finding other ways to process this. It's investing in *yourself*. It's rediscovering the parts of you that have been consumed by this chaos. And remembering that when all of this is burned to the ground, *you* will rise—like the Phoenix that you are. You will navigate this world with grace, laughter, joy, and love. Manifest that. Manifest the carefree, dancing, laughing, intelligent parts of you that have been buried under all this pain."

I begin to cry.

I sit in gratitude, recognizing how fucking lucky I am to have people who support me, who say the things I *don't* want to hear but *need* to.

For a moment, I remember—my husband used to be that for me.

Then, I stare out the window.

9/10/22

SHARE THE RECEIPTS

"Be kind, for everyone you meet is fighting a hard battle."
~ Plato

On September 10th, 2022, I meet up with two girlfriends for a birthday brunch at a charming café in the West Village. With my mother staying at my place, I feel comfortable leaving Jude for a few hours. Still, it feels strange driving into the city alone, just me and my thoughts.

I never imagined I'd be going through a divorce on my 38th birthday—who would? I'm not exactly *sad*; I just feel...off. Maybe it's because the *other woman* celebrated her birthday just four days earlier—almost exactly ten years younger than me. Weird indeed.

As traffic slows, I catch my reflection in the rearview mirror, tracing the lines etched between my brows, the soft creases at the corners of my eyes—evidence of too many tears. I think back to myself a decade ago. While I prefer how I look now, I can't help but wonder: Will I become less desirable the closer I get to 40? Even though I know I'm a catch, I also know the narrative—*the aging, nagging ball-and-chain, left for a younger woman.* What a cliché.

My eyes begin to pool with tears, but I stop myself. I *refuse* to indulge in this story today. This is *my* day, and I won't let *him* steal my joy for another second. And I sure as hell won't steal my *own* joy by picking myself apart.

I pull up to the café and park directly in front of a fire hydrant. *Whatever.* The worst has already happened—I give zero fucks. My friends are already seated outside, and I can *feel* their disapproval as I cross the cobblestone street.

"Mere, you're going to get a ticket," Anya warns, watching me with narrowed eyes.

"Who cares?" I shrug, grinning.

Her face twists in concern, so I soften. "I'll keep an eye on it, don't worry."

We sip iced lattes and mimosas, laughing between bites of avocado toast and eggs Benedict. Then, midway through the meal, Anya leans in and lowers her voice.

"Isn't that that one model?"

I follow her gaze over my shoulder.

And there she is.

Emily Ratajkowski. *Yes,* that Emily Ratajkowski. *Emrata.*

Even with oversized black sunglasses covering her chocolate eyes, I know it's her. She's standing just a few feet away.

I turn back to my friends, my voice hushed but firm. "That's Emily Ratajkowski. She's not just a model—she's an *incredible* writer. You guys, her book means so much to me. I want to tell her, but I don't want to creep her out."

My friends don't hesitate. "Go."

And so, I do.

As I approach, I feel *no nerves.* In fact, it's almost déjà vu, as if I've lived this moment before. She's standing on the corner with a friend while her sweet baby boy sits quietly in his stroller, waiting for a table.

"Hi, Emily," I say gently. "I won't keep you long, I just wanted to tell you—I love your book. I *hope* you'll be putting out more of your work. You're brilliant. I've made so many people read it, and they all feel the same. You are *truly* inspiring to me—for so many reasons."

She pushes her sunglasses up onto her head, tucking her hair behind her ears, and suddenly, her eyes well with tears. She wipes them away with her sleeve.

"I can't believe I'm crying," she says, laughing through the emotion. "It must be my PMS making me so emotional."

Without thinking, I say, "I'm going through what you are. And I have a little boy too."

Her expression shifts, softens.

"How old is he?" she asks.

"He's four and just the absolute sweetest," I reply.

We continue talking about our boys and the strange, disorienting experience of suddenly doing it all *alone*. We share a few more tears over the heartbreak, the shock, the adjustment. Before parting, she wishes me a happy birthday and waves to my friends as I head back to the table.

Wow, I think, grinning widely. *Even in the middle of the most horrible shit, random awesome things can still happen.*

That evening, when I get home, I do what anyone would—I Google Emily.

The headlines confirm it: she filed for divorce *two days ago.*

Maybe her tears were from PMS. Maybe they were from my words.

But more than likely, it was the grief of having to live a life she never thought she'd have to.

TEN DAYS LATER, on September 20th, 2022, *Adam Levine* has his own cheating scandal. His former mistress, Sumner Stroh—a young Instagram model—releases text exchanges between them, exposing their affair. It happened during his marriage to Behati Prinsloo, the South African model.

One message stands out. Levine asks if she'd be *okay* with him naming his unborn child *Sumner*—if it were a boy.

Luckily for everyone involved, the baby was a girl. Within minutes of each other, two of my closest friends send me the same tweet:

> "AFTER ADAM LEVINE CHEATING ON HIS WIFE LET'S REMEMBER & NORMALIZE THE FACT THAT CHEATING WAS NEVER ABOUT A WOMAN'S LACK OF BEAUTY, WORTH OR ANYTHING FOR THAT MATTER BUT INSTEAD A MAN'S ABUNDANCE OF INSECURITIES, UNWORTHINESS & DESPERATION. DON'T LET MEN MANIPULATE THAT REALITY." ~ SHENNA, TWITTER.COM

My friends *know* I need to hear this. They know I need to be reminded of *the truth*. Because in my lowest moments—those moments of *untruth*—self-doubt, comparison, and the gnawing feeling of *not being enough* creep in.

Remy texts me:

"That tweet is exactly what I've been feeling about you. It has *nothing* to do with you or even *her*. It's his own inner demons and self-loathing. I *hate* when people say, 'Can you believe he cheated on *her*?! She's gorgeous!' It feeds the idea that our worth is tied to how we look. It's so antiquated. The *least* interesting thing about us is our appearance. And I have to remind myself of that every day because life tries to convince us otherwise."

I think about Levine—how *even with everything*—the fame, the money, the adoration, the wife, the children, the *full life*—he still *found time* to start communicating with Sumner.

And even *after months* of not speaking, he still reached out. To *check in*. To see if naming his *child* after her would be *okay*.

MY MIND DRIFTS TO BEHATI.

What did she feel when she saw that message? Had they ever

even considered *that* name for their child? If it was true, did she think back to the moment it first came up? Who suggested it? Were they lying naked together, hands resting over the small swell of her stomach, embracing the excitement of their growing family—when he spoke the name of his mistress?

Even if it was all a lie, a perfectly crafted manipulation to tempt Sumner into contact again, did a disagreement with Behati propel him to seek his *fix* elsewhere? Did Behati, like me, look at the date of that message and start scanning her emails, her texts—piecing together *exactly* where she was at that moment?

The *cliché* makes me sick. And worse, my own connection to it fills me with rage.

In a petty, impulsive act of defiance, I grab my phone and open my ex's Spotify account. I change the title of one of his playlists to: **"No Fallopian Tubes = No Longer Needed."**

Then, in the description, I leave him a little poem:

41-28 = 13 years apart... what a cliché. You used to say you'd always stay, no young thing would pull you astray. But it's a cold day in hell with the truth laid bare—someone close to your baby sister's age. So in denial, leaves fatherless child, while you go out to prey.

I hit save and close the app with a satisfied click.
Then, the rage simmers.
And I scroll.
Back through my texts. Back to *that* day.
The day he bought the Plan B.
7/22/22. 9:20 AM.
At 8:48 AM, he texted me: "Did he get on the bus okay?"

He *never* texted that late. Usually, he'd ask before our son left for summer school at 7:50 AM. I remember feeling relieved that he checked in, but also... surprised. Why didn't he try to put our son on the bus himself? He had just gotten out of rehab. He was staying nearby. Wasn't he *desperate* to be a father again?

Something had felt *off* that morning. A subtle, nagging unease.

And now, I wonder: *When were they having sex?* Was it at night, so intense that they overslept, missing our son's bus ride altogether from sheer exhaustion? Were they climaxing just as I was chasing our son to brush his hair and teeth before scrambling outside?

I wonder if he finished inside her and then went to pee right after—like he always did with me. Did he even shower before heading to the drugstore to pick up the Plan B? What came first: the disclosure that she wasn't on birth control, followed by the agreement to use Plan B, or did they rip off the condom in the heat of passion? Was the risk of pregnancy an afterthought?

What was their conversation like when he went to get the pill? Or did she tag along, a thrill running through her at the thought of sleeping with a married man?

And with that, I wonder why my mind keeps returning to her. The "other woman" owes me nothing. *He* does. *He* should be my focus. So why am I obsessed with analyzing *her*, critiquing *her*? Why do I want to expose her, to shame her in front of her friends, to even scold them for standing by her?

Why am I jealous?

True to form, I confide in my friend Leigh, hoping she'll help me make sense of this feeling—hoping she'll wash me clean of it. In truth, she can't. But she does validate my feelings with the following:

> "It makes sense that you'd feel jealous," Leigh says. "Instead of putting his energy into improving himself or repairing your marriage, he chose the easy way out—a temporary Band-Aid fix in the form of sex with someone else. Remember, this isn't about her. It's about his insecurity, his mental health, his narrow-mindedness, and his inability to see the impact of his actions on you and your son."
>
> "Addicts focus most on whatever will immediately make them feel good—they don't see beyond that. That's exactly what he did. He wasn't thinking about consequences, about anything past that

moment. This is about Tripp. Not her. He's the one who's fucked up. He's the one who's made selfish, shitty choices with zero awareness of how his actions affect others—especially you. He can't cope with real-life stressors in any healthy way. So he takes the path of least resistance, whatever gives him the quickest relief. When life got hard, when he actually had to work for something, he bailed."

Leigh's words feel like clarity. And I realize: I've been conditioned to hate the woman first and the man second.

Society has trained us to hate other women—we've been pitted against each other since...forever. I think of EmRata writing about how Ben Affleck suggested her for *Gone Girl* when David Fincher wanted a star "men were obsessed with and women hate."

Ironically, Emily Ratajkowski later weighed in on the Adam Levine cheating scandal, calling out the very conditioning that still makes me critique my husband's paramour. Even though she appeared in Maroon 5's *Love Somebody* music video, that didn't stop her from speaking out—**not** against Levine's mistress, but against the people (especially women) attacking her online.

This is why Emily is a badass.

She calls out the "skewed power dynamic" Levine exploited and condemns his behavior as "predatory and manipulative." In a TikTok video, she says:

"I don't understand why we continue to blame women for men's mistakes, especially when you're talking about 20-something-year-old women dealing with men in positions of power who are twice their age."

Damn. I'm guilty.

Emily goes on, calling the backlash against the women involved "classic misogyny."

"If you're the one in a relationship, you're the one who's obligated to be

loyal. So the whole other woman, 'They're to blame,' that's bad and it's literally designed to keep women apart."

Truth. Fuck.

"If you have receipts, share them, you're doing other ladies a favor."

Yes, Em. I can vouch for that. Share the receipts, so the wife doesn't have to find them. 😃

9/21/22

ALLY

"If you shut up truth, and bury it underground, it will but grow" ~ Emile Zola

My best friend, Remy, has finally arrived. *Thank God.* She flew into NYC to celebrate her 10th wedding anniversary, but before her husband gets here, we're spending a night on the town—kicking it off at Harry Styles' last performance at Madison Square Garden.

With a boa draped over my plaid jumpsuit, I drive down the FDR, buzzing with excitement—until my phone rings.

It's my mom.

"Mere, a new social worker has been assigned to the case. She just left," she says quickly.

Time stops. Everything goes dark. My breath catches, and my eyes slam shut.

"Mere, are you there?"

My mom's voice jolts me back. My eyes snap open—I'm just entering a tunnel. But the weight of the darkness feels suffocating. One hand grips the steering wheel, the other clutches my chest.

The Plan B Chronicles

"Don't worry," my mom reassures me. "She was very kind. The opposite of Stacy."

Hearing Stacy's name makes my stomach churn.

Last week, when I finally stopped obsessively checking the phone records, I noticed something: Stacy—the fucking Child Protective Services social worker—was texting my husband until 11 p.m. one night.

At any other time in my life, I would have immediately contacted her agency about how wildly unprofessional that was. But I was too exhausted, too distraught, too depleted to summon my usual fire for justice.

Now, my mom explains that the new social worker, Evelyn, just interviewed her and is trying to get in touch with me. My whole body trembles, nausea surging, as I force myself to focus on the road—anything to avoid veering into another car.

I call Evelyn back immediately.

"I don't understand," I tell her. "Stacy told me the case was closed on Wednesday."

Evelyn sighs. Stacy never submitted her investigation. She left out key information.

That horrible gut feeling about her flares up again.

I unload everything on Evelyn: how Stacy made comments about my sex life, how she dismissed my concerns about STDs, how she reprimanded me for not submitting proof that I'd been in therapy—even though I was never asked for it. (And when I did provide it? She made sure I knew my husband had already submitted *his* treatment updates on time.) The entire experience made me feel like I was the one under investigation.

Then, I drop the bombshell:

"After reviewing the phone records, I found out that Stacy and my husband were texting late at night."

Silence.

Evelyn is stunned. And then—validation.

"I'm so sorry," she says. "That was completely inappropriate and unethical."

Finally. A woman from the outside sees my truth.

9/22/22

HELL'S KITCHEN

"A wise man hears one word and understands two" ~
Edgar Allan Poe

o you have a few minutes? I want to talk to you about something," Maria, our nanny, asked one fateful day in the fall of 2021.

Ugh, what now? Is she quitting? Did something happen? She's only been with us for two months!

"Yeah, of course. I'm free now," I said as we walked to the back of the house and sat down.

Maria was—and still is—one of a kind. She loves children and a clean house. From the moment she started working with our son that fall, she immediately meshed with our family, taking charge of the cleaning without even being asked. And since I was drowning in household responsibilities, having another set of hands (and eyes) felt like a godsend.

Born and raised in the Bronx, Maria is a straight shooter. She has no problem telling it like it is, and I had always deeply appreciated that about her. Until that day.

"I wanted to know if you have any concerns about your husband's... whereabouts," Maria said, her tone serious.

"What do you mean?" I asked, confused. I *knew* he was at work.

"The long hours. Coming home late. You know... there could be funny business," she said, as it dawned on me what she was implying.

"Maria, nooo, nooo, he's not doing anything like that," I laughed. "This is just part of the job. TV shows have crazy hours—it's the nature of the business. He wouldn't cheat. He's not that kind of guy."

I truly believed my words.

Maria sat there, watching me, her expression serious as I tried to convince her—and myself—that my husband was exactly who I thought he was.

I knew Maria's history. Her marriage had ended in infidelity—her ex had carried on a long affair with their neighbor, always finding excuses to stay out later and later. She had been naïve, trusting, until she found the pictures on his phone. I assumed her past was coloring how she saw my marriage. That my husband's late nights triggered her, causing her to project her own experience onto me.

A few hours later, I texted Remy to get her read on the conversation.

"Umm, that's really inappropriate, Mere. That's crossing a line," she wrote back, shocked. "Does Tripp know she said that?"

"No. I don't think I'll mention it to him. He's been super reactive lately, and I can't risk losing Maria."

The truth was, his alcoholism had been getting worse, and no one—not even him—knew how bad it really was. I had started to parent **more** with Maria, and deep down, I knew that our son was safer with her.

MORNING. **9/22/22**

Hindsight. Maria tried to warn me, but I brushed it off—too desperate to believe that everything was fine. Sitting here now, I see how hard that must have been for her, watching me walk the same path she once stumbled through.

She has lived this before: the long nights, the quiet lies, the slow unraveling of trust. And now, here she is, watching it happen again—this time to me. It's like her past is replaying itself, and she's stuck on the sidelines, powerless to change the ending.

I wonder what she saw in my face that day. Did I remind her of the naïve hope she once clung to? It must have been agonizing for her to relive her own mistakes while I dismissed her warning. And yet, she stayed. *Steady. Present.* Almost as if she knew I'd need her when the truth finally crushed me.

We made a deal: as long as I keep her stocked with Dunkin' Donuts coffee and coffee cake, she'll discount the childcare. But the reality is, Maria is caring for more than just Jude—she's caring for me, too. She brings me food while I work, constantly reminding me to eat.

I have become so thin. My ribs protrude from starvation.

It's not intentional; I just have zero appetite. I am sick over all of it—everything seen and unseen.

I wish I could go back to that day when she sat me down. I wish I had believed her.

But I also wish I could be that same naïve person again, the one who still believed in the good of people. The one who still had the "that couldn't happen to me" feeling I once took for granted.

I am forever changed.

I will never be so trusting again.

NIGHT. 9/22/22 - The Dream

Heights are my biggest fear, and here I am, being led to the top of a high-rise building. I'm reassured that it will be worth it. My legs turn to jelly, my heart pounds, but I breathe deeply, reminding myself I'm safe with the person I love.

I hold their hand tightly, step into the sun, and the view is breathtaking. I loosen my grip, finally relaxing.

Suddenly, I'm pushed off the side of the building.

I'm falling. There's nothing beneath me. The speed of the fall feels like my skin is being ripped from my body. I reach out desperately, grasping for anything to save me, but there's nothing. My lungs feel crushed, incapable of releasing a scream.

Then, I hit the concrete. My heart explodes on the pavement, my insides spilling out in all directions. A woman's trench coat is soaked with my blood. Another person removes their jacket to cover the ruin of my body.

My soul escapes its broken container, seeking my killer. Invisible, I watch them step into the elevator, calm and collected. No tears. The elevator doors close, and they pull out their phone—scrolling Grubhub, casually deciding what lunch they'd like to have delivered to their apartment in Hell's Kitchen.

10/1/22

NEW LIPS

"In every picture there should be shade as well as light" ~ James Boswell

I notice his lips are full as they eagerly touch mine. I like how they feel, but they're unfamiliar, and I keep trying to adjust to their movement. While striving to remember how to kiss, I almost find a rhythm, but as soon as I do, I feel a hint of tongue and pull away.

"Hey, I said I want gentle, no tongue kisses, remember?" I say with a smirk, locking eyes with him as I playfully set my limits.

I can see my limits excite him. He nods, a devilish grin spreading across his face, and without hesitation, he goes back to kissing me. I feel the weight of my hair nestled between his fingers as he holds the back of my neck, slowing down his kisses, honoring my request.

I soak in this moment. It feels nice to be touched, to be desired.

He smells clean, and as I touch the back of his neck, pulling him closer, I can tell his hair is freshly cut—soft bristles under my fingers. I move my hand back and forth on his neck, feeling the contrast between his smooth skin and the hairline. This is a familiar feeling; I know how to do this.

After reminding him I need to relieve the babysitter, he walks me to my car, fingers interlaced with mine.

He's holding my hand, I think to myself. Suddenly, a surge of concern rises. *Am I supposed to be doing this? Should I?* But the fear quickly passes as I remember I'm single.

He switches hands, placing one on my lower back, his arm crossing over his torso to ensure I'm holding the other. I ease into his embrace, enjoying the feeling of care and protection.

Before I drive off, he jumps into the car and looks at me.

"I really like you, and I want to see you again. Whatever time or day works for you, I'll make it happen," he says, his sincerity overwhelming.

I look away, blushing, shocked by his bluntness. This transparency is foreign to me. I glance back into his chocolate eyes and reply, "I like you too."

He shuts the door, and I feel a rush of excitement. I drive off, smiling, but as I make a right turn, his silhouette fades in my rearview mirror. Suddenly, I begin to sob—uncontrollable, hard tears that hit the steering wheel. I'm stunned as I witness my body's sadness, leaving me, spilling outside of me.

Memories flood me. Flashes of intimate moments invade my mind without warning. Memories of when my husband held my hand with care. Of when I would stroke the back of his neck. Of how he smelled clean and like himself, instead of the stench of cologne masking alcohol.

I sob for myself. Life doesn't feel real; it feels like a movie, and I haven't decided if I want to be in it because I didn't write this script. I sob because I'm angry I even have to navigate a new kiss. I thought I'd be kissing the same lips all my life. I sob for the loss of comfort, for the ease of knowing every movement of my partner, my lover. I miss my husband.

Then, as quickly as it comes, I hate him, and rage fills my body.

My tears turn to acid. The man who was my biggest protector is now my biggest betrayer.

"How could he? How could he?" I repeat to myself. I didn't choose this. I don't want to be here, kissing a stranger.

A vision of them kissing invades my mind, so vivid it feels like my brain is being burned by it. He initiated the kiss with her just like my date did with me tonight. My husband chose to kiss her while I was home, caring for our son. He chose this.

Just as quickly as the rage fills me, a wave of calm pours over me when I remember how direct my date was about his intentions. I realize that there are people out there who will match my transparency. I was candid about my life, and that felt refreshing. This is what the truth feels like. This is what I deserve.

As my tears dry and my rage dissipates, I know—I will be okay. I want to live in truth and transparency, not secrecy and lies. No matter what happens, I will only engage with people who desire the same—the ones who crave truth.

Part III

"Fall if you will, but rise you must." ~ James Joyce

10/25/22

DISSOCIATION

"Difficulty comes from our lack of confidence" ~ Seneca

Two weeks ago, I kissed a stranger for the first time, fumbling to match his movements, adjusting to the unfamiliar rhythm of his touch. Today, I'll stand face-to-face with another stranger—the man I once knew intimately but can no longer recognize.

The smoke of sage spirals around me as I prepare for family court. This will be the first time seeing my husband in three months, and I'm trying everything to calm my mind and protect my energy.

Amid the chaos, I've leaned into anything spiritual or healing: crystals, prayer, cleansing baths, healing spices. All I know is that no one truly understands why or what is happening in the world, and for that reason, I'm surrendering. No more judgment. I'm open to anything that can help me get through this time.

My friend Elara will attend court with me, and I'm incredibly grateful. She's a particular type of friend—one where a month can go by without speaking, yet we pick up right where we left off, on the same page. We dislike surface-level conversation and prefer to dive deep immediately.

There's a connective synergy between us. Nothing needs to be spoken; we just feel it. I swear Elara gives me power. When she tells me it'll be okay, *I know it will.*

After we ride up the elevator to the court lobby, pass through the metal detector, and clasp hands, we finally find my attorney, Celeste. Though small in stature, Celeste is poised, calm, and—most importantly—sharp. She's studying my paperwork in a tiny conference room. After a quick check-in, we're instructed to sit in the lobby.

As we turn the corner, *there he is.*

I squeeze Elara's hand as I see the back of my 6'4" husband, looking out the window over the city. We sit down on the bench in the aisle next to him. He's just a few feet away, on the other side of a partition. We aren't allowed to speak due to the protection order, and we are about to go before the judge to discuss visitation.

At this moment, everything feels surreal. I ask Elara, "Is this really happening? This feels like a movie." She validates my feelings and says she's feeling the same.

"I think I'm dissociating, too," she whispers, so my husband won't hear.

Time stands still. Our surroundings feel fake and frozen, as if we're not part of them at all, but instead observing them—like being in a simulation.

The man who held my legs while I pushed our son into this world is sitting on the other side of a flimsy, man-made partition. The man who destroyed me emotionally and financially sits just a few feet away. Every instinct to run to him matches an equally powerful instinct to run away. The burden of this contradiction is so great.

"This is so painful," I whisper to Elara. She shakes her head in disbelief. No one saw this change in him coming. That helps me not feel quite as foolish as I have. Knowing that others were just as shocked as I was soothes me in some strange way.

"Ohhh, snap!" a loud voice shouts, echoing off the lobby walls.

"Oh my god, that's his lawyer," I tell Elara. I hate this man. The day before, Merrick (of course, his name is Merrick) told my lawyer, "Nothing even happened," and that they wouldn't respond to the proposed divorce terms because they're "so unreasonable, they don't warrant a response."

We hear Merrick start chatting with Tripp, and the voice I once loved hits my eardrum, causing me to wince. It's different. Maybe it's just been a while since I've heard it, or maybe it's because it *is* different—it's forever changed.

As I focus on my husband's voice, I'm suddenly pulled out of my thoughts when Merrick steps in front of us, expecting us to stand. He's a wrinkled white man with even whiter hair, likely in his 60s. Loud, attention-seeking, always acting like everyone's best friend.

"Don't be afraid, I'm nice, I'm nice, I swear, I won't bite," he says condescendingly, looking down at us as we remain seated.

I give him a blank stare, tightening my grip on Elara's hand.

"Want to go talk?" he says in his thick New York accent, directing his gaze at Elara.

"No. No, I don't," she replies.

"You won't even step aside to discuss this?" he asks, his voice raised, brows furrowed with intensity. "Don't you want this to be resolved?" He continues aggressively.

The man has clearly never picked up on a social cue in his life. Rather, he thrives on confrontation; you can feel it. He gets off on it.

"This isn't my lawyer; this is my friend," I state firmly.

He steps back, laughing, his stomach shaking as he tosses his head back, cackling. He thinks this is the funniest thing in the world based on his theatrics. He finds it absolutely hilarious; I think it's just idiotic. Do most people hold hands with their lawyer? What a fucking idiot.

He plods away, still laughing, soaking in the attention from the guards as he recounts his ridiculous misstep. Finally, thank God, he goes into the conference room with my lawyer. Elara and I make eye contact, hearing his "lawyer's voice" raised and intense, muffled through the thick walls and shut door.

Then, someone calls out our last names.

"Stanley vs. Beardmore, the judge is now ready to see you," an officer announces.

Only the lawyers enter first, and they're in there for only a few minutes.

"The case was dismissed. It will go to criminal court because it wasn't filed as a matrimonial case," my lawyer informs me.

"So, what now?" I ask.

My lawyer explains that she'll use this time to discuss a possible settlement with... Merrick. Elara and I sit in the hallway, far from my ex.

A few minutes pass, and my lawyer comes back down the hall to meet us.

"That was fast," I say as she shakes her head.

"I don't negotiate with people that bombastic," she states.

I'm pissed. I feel enraged on her behalf. She was subjected to his wrath while trying to help me, and he doubled down, claiming "nothing" happened to me. I suggest we email Tripp's lawyer the drug tests so he can understand the severity of the situation—that there's no "nothing" when a child is involved.

Just then, his lawyer loudly walks down the hall, making sure everyone in the building hears him say,

"Okay, okay! Let's calm down, stay calm, and talk through this matter."

My blood boils.

"Ohhh, yeah, *she's* the one that needs to calm down," I mutter, as my lawyer walks back with him to the conference room. He's shifting the blame onto Celeste to make himself look good—maybe to the guards? What an entitled piece of shit.

Elara is reacting too. She's triggered by his dominating tone, his overwhelming "Trump vibe," and his obvious tactics to project, blame shift, and gaslight.

My lawyer comes back quickly. She informs me that she presented the drug analysis, which Merrick claimed he's "never seen." But there was no change in his stance—he still thought I was "ridiculous and unreasonable."

His critique of me is one thing, but his treatment of my attorney sends me over the edge. I've always been able to advocate for others more than for myself. I wonder why that is because it's not working for me now. If I had put my own needs first in the past, I might not even be in this predicament.

But something shifts in me as I ask, "Can I meet with him? I want to talk to this guy."

Elara and my attorney exchange shocked looks. I was shaky and fearful when I entered the courthouse this morning—nauseous, dizzy, the whole deal. But now, I'm just ready to deal with this prick.

"Tripp will also be present. Do you think you can handle that?" my attorney asks.

"Yes," I reply confidently.

"Are you sure, Mere?" Elara asks, worry lacing her voice.

"Yes, let's do this," I state, ready to pounce.

10/25/22

BULLY

"My tongue will tell the anger of my heart, or else my heart, concealing it, will break" ~ William Shakespeare

The walls are white, but the room is small—maybe seven by seven feet. I'm directly facing Merrick, and Tripp sits next to him. While Tripp does appear sober, he's gained a lot of weight; he looks puffy and old—not in a good way. I mention that because, as most aging men go, they're often described as "ruggedly handsome," as if aging only makes them more desirable. Meanwhile, women become invisible as they age.

As we lock eyes, Tripp tries his best puppy dog face, but it's too intense, and I quickly look away.

Our lawyers decide to begin with the finances.

Merrick starts, "I'm not sure you understand that if we go to court, you'll get much less than you're asking. Can you come down?"

He's referring to the $1,700 a month in child support I've requested—a fraction of what he was contributing before this.

"This man decimated me financially," I snap. "We were just

about to buy the home we'd been renting for four years, the one our son is comfortable in. Did Tripp tell you I did everything to get the pre-approval for the house? Did he tell you we were about to buy it from our landlord? That we had two tenants lined up to essentially pay our mortgage, and we would have been living for free?"

Merrick just stares at me, expressionless.

"Did he tell you he spent all our money on drugs and alcohol? That he'd rage against me when I finally stopped loaning him money, even though he makes significantly more than me? He was drinking a handle of vodka a day and popping five to eight Adderall pills a day, buying them from his drug dealer for $15 a pill. Why don't you do the math and tell me why he can't afford $1,700 a month in child support? I'm the unreasonable one, right, Merrick?"

"No, you're unreasonable because you want Tripp to help pay for rent until your son is 26 years old," Merrick interrupts.

"Do you not understand my son is on the spectrum?" I shoot back. "We have no idea if he'll be able to live on his own when he turns 18. That's why that's in place. The law states that a child with a disability will be supported until they're 26 in cases like this. I know Tripp doesn't believe our son is autistic, but he is. He has a disability. By law, Tripp is required to help support him. Just because Tripp doesn't want to face this doesn't mean it isn't real. I have to keep a calm environment for our child and provide everything he needs. Tripp has no idea what it takes to parent a child with a disability."

"There's the bully," Tripp states.

I shut down at those three words. A sensation overwhelms my body, like my bones can't carry the weight of my skin. I just want to lay down and sleep.

"Okay, let's go; I'm done," I say to my lawyer, as tears begin to pour out.

"No, no, let's let her talk. You be quiet, Tripp," Merrick surprisingly interjects.

I sit there, crying, in disbelief that he could ever call me a bully when that's exactly what he's been doing to me. Advocating for myself and telling my story is now being a bully.

I wipe away more tears and focus on my breath to center myself again.

"I'm trying my best to stay calm, but so much has happened that I don't think you know. I've been trying to maintain a calm environment for our son, putting Jude first while Tripp puts *himself* first. Unfortunately, Tripp left detox before completing it, came home, and didn't sleep. When I pleaded with him to go back to rehab—which he refused—I then asked for a separation to show I was serious. How did he respond? He kicked a steel baby-gate at me, nearly breaking my wrist."

"I called the cops on myself because I was worried," Tripp interrupts.

"And I didn't press charges, remember? Instead, I was so concerned for your mental health that I convinced the police to take you to the hospital for a mental evaluation. I refused medical care because I didn't want our son to wake up to a police officer and no parents there. Do you understand how scary that would be for a child? Do you know what it's like to watch police officers enter your home and walk around your bed to make sure your child is safe?"

I can feel my voice rising, my anger growing as I remember that awful night. I'm infuriated that Tripp brought up calling the cops. He almost seems to boast about it, as if it proves he's a "good guy"—someone who did the "right" thing in a tough situation. He speaks as though calling the cops cancels out the reason they were called—the violence.

"Our son is on the autism spectrum, which Tripp still doesn't believe because I was 'looking for something,' accusing me of wanting our child to have something wrong with him. Did he tell you that he drove drunk with our son?"

Merrick just stares. Tripp looks down, not meeting my eyes.

"No? I guess I'm just irrational, like you've told my lawyer multiple times. Do you know what I see as irrational, Merrick? Tripp would come to our house reeking of weed at 9 am, to spend time with Jude after rehab. I guess *I'm* irrational because, even knowing this, I let him stay over one night. But instead of waking up to his family, which he insisted he wanted to keep intact, he got up at 2 am and left. Jude and I woke up to find his daddy gone, because he couldn't 'sleep'... But yes, clearly *I'm* the irrational one."

Tripp is visibly wiping away tears, but he knows it's the truth.

"Again, this is after rehab. After. Tripp agreed to go straight to sober living but didn't. What's interesting is I wasn't allowed to ask why; I was treated as if it was preposterous to even ask. I arranged to have a car pick him up from sober living to go to intensive outpatient every day—the recommended step down after rehab. He refused and returned to our home, even though he wasn't supposed to. When I returned from Ohio a week later, I asked him to stay at a hotel because he was using again. And all he did was make me feel bad for him. I wasn't a supportive wife, he didn't have money. I *did* feel bad for him, so bad, that I covered the bills for the family. I paid the rent in July and August, all while he lived at his mistress's apartment without my knowledge."

Merrick doesn't flinch. No reaction. No emotion. Tripp wipes away more tears, looking down.

"Did you know that I had to get STD testing? Do you know what it's like to say it's because my husband is cheating on me? I found the Plan B receipt in his car the morning he came over and became violent again. Let's talk about that day. I emailed him that morning, asking for separation again, to which he texted me, 'We are not separating.' This man had slept with another woman the day before, but he was going to tell me that we were not separating. Then, he proceeds to say that he's coming over. I asked that he come over at 2 pm so our son's nap wouldn't be interrupted. He called and said he was coming over right now and that he'd be taking Jude for a bike ride. I could tell he was fucked up by the way he sounded. You can say the cops were called over a difference between 1 pm and 2 pm. You can minimize my concerns, but I wasn't going to let him take our son and put his life in danger—not on my watch. Tripp had keys to the apartment but still chose to kick down the door and destroy the doorframe. He knew my 68-year-old mother, our son, and I were on the other side of that door, so what was the need for that force? Do you understand how scary that was for us? Calling the police was what I had to do, not what I wanted to do. But it was 'nothing,' right, Merrick? I was just hysterical and irrational, right? How dare you speak of me like this to my lawyer, over and over, and yell at her like you did today."

I know exactly what I'm doing by repeating Merrick's name, but it has to be done. Merrick has emboldened Tripp's delusions, which is why we're even in court in the first place. Tripp has convinced himself that he's justified, and Merrick has fanned his anger toward me, painting me as a "maniacal woman." And though I've gotten some of it, Celeste has taken the brunt of it, unjustly so.

"I'm very sorry for the way that I spoke about you to your lawyer before having the facts. I'm sorry I raised my voice at your lawyer. I only had some of the facts. I'm sorry. Can we now please try to make some movement here?"

I stare at Merrick, analyzing his expression, seeking sincerity. But I can smell it on him—he's placating me. I know it, but he doesn't think I do. Despite it, I realize that rehashing the trauma would be in vain and possibly more harmful to my nervous system. No compassion would be generated for me. It isn't worth it. So, I nod.

10/25/22

HONEY

"Pride and excess bring disaster for man" ~ Xunzi

"You know that if we took you to court, you wouldn't get nearly that amount," Merrick says as he stands up, cracking open a piece of Nicorette and popping it into his mouth like he's some "cool guy."

"I understand, but considering the circumstances…" I begin.

"The circumstances don't matter in the court of law," Merrick yells, cutting me off.

I breathe deeply, trying to stay calm and not react to the interruptions and yelling, but I can feel myself shutting down again.

"…I understand, but I was hoping my husband would think about me and do right by his family. I can't imagine putting someone through this and thinking, 'you get the bare minimum,'" I say, my voice tinged with frustration.

The more we hash out the terms of the divorce, the more agitated Merrick becomes. Finally, something strange happens: Merrick becomes even more argumentative, and I notice Tripp trying to talk down his lawyer. It's as if Tripp realizes his lawyer may have led him down the wrong path by bringing us here.

As we negotiate, Merrick and Tripp keep stepping out of the room to keep the conversations between my lawyer and me private. My lawyer remains stoic, focused ahead. We watch as Merrick walks back in; he pauses at the door, looking back at Tripp. I can hear Merrick saying,

"...Sassy, but she is gorgeous. She is gorgeous, right?" followed by his cackling.

"Celeste, are they talking about my appearance?" I ask, keeping my eyes on them.

"Yes, I believe they are," she responds without meeting my gaze.

"Wow," I say out loud.

"*The audacity*," repeats in my mind, over and over again. The audacity to discuss my appearance is mind-blowing. The audacity to label the recounting of my trauma as "sassy." The audacity to belittle me in both my inner and outward expressions of self is repulsive. A sensation rises from my chest into my throat. I'm not sure whether I want to choke, throw up, scream, or cry. It feels like one simultaneous *sense*. This isn't new for me; it isn't for most women. Having their appearance and conduct discussed by men is *commonplace*. So, I shouldn't even be surprised.

We're able to agree on custody and child support during the interim until we can finalize the divorce.

As they leave, I stop Tripp and say, "Before your addiction took over, the person you were never would've hired someone like him. You never would've let a man speak to me that way."

"I know, honey. This is just lawyer stuff. Let's go, Merrick," Tripp says as he walks out the door.

Honey.

The word lands in my chest like a spark, igniting a flame of anger that burns hotter than anything Merrick or his cackling could ever muster. *Honey*. As if we're still playing house. As if the betrayal, the lies, and the destruction he brought into our lives could be smoothed over with a casual, condescending term of endearment. *Honey.* The man who let me drown while he swam away, who let a stranger belittle me in my most vulnerable moment, has the nerve to call me honey.

I sit there, staring at the door as it swings shut behind him, and the simultaneous sensation—choking, screaming, crying—starts to fade. One thought remains, sharp and clear:

I'm not your Honey.

10/29/22

PLAN B

"The beginning is always today" ~ Mary Wollstonecraft

It's Saturday morning, and I'm in line at CVS. Jude is decked out in a skeleton costume, running back and forth through the aisles behind me. It's been 15 minutes of waiting for my prescription, and I gave up on being a good parent five minutes in.

The chronic stress I've endured has impacted my memory, and I can't find my Zoloft prescription anywhere. I had to contact my psychiatrist, explain the whole situation, and go back and forth with the pharmacy. The last sentence makes it sound like a short series of events, when in fact, it spanned two days, meaning I missed two days of pills.

During the divorce proceedings, my psychiatrist recommended increasing my Zoloft dosage. I didn't think it was totally necessary, but I agreed. In the past, missing a pill or two wasn't a big deal, but today? I feel like I have the flu. Dizziness and body aches have me struggling. I hope I'll feel better once the pill gets into my system—I'm rallying to get to "Boo at the Zoo" with my friend Leigh and her family. Even though seeing intact families at the zoo might not be the best for my mental health, I need my friends, and I need Jude to have normalcy.

Anyway, back to CVS. I'm still in line, hunched over from the dizziness, trying a trick for fighting it by putting my head between my legs for a few moments. As the dizziness passes, I'm at eye level with the magazine section. I glance to the left and see a box labeled "Plan B Emergency Contraception." It's in a clear plastic case, requiring a CVS employee to unlock it before purchase. A mix of nausea, sadness, and heat washes over me. It isn't a light splash of these feelings; it's a fucking tsunami.

Suddenly, I'm transported back to the day I found the receipt. I can smell the stench of the car, feel the hot leather seats on the back of my legs. I see the trash in the car, the coins in the console, and the 5-Hour Energy bottle as I try to piece together why my husband would have a receipt for Plan B in his car.

"Mommy!" Jude shouts as he climbs on my back, pulling me out of my mind and back into my reality, which doesn't feel like reality at all.

"Ma'am, your prescription is ready," the cashier says, looking down at me with annoyance. It's clear she wants my unruly child and sick self to get out of there.

I pull myself up to the counter to pay, aware that the Plan B box is near my right foot. I feel its energy, its taunting words: *"I'm down here, Meredith."* It sounds like Isla Fisher's character in *Wedding Crashers* when she says, "I found yooouuu," in that psychotic, childish voice.

"So, do you sell a lot of those Plan Bs?" I blurt out to the cashier. She gives me a little smirk—a nice change from her annoyance.

"We're usually sold out," she says almost proudly.

"Oh, today must be my lucky day," I mutter sarcastically.

"Do you need me to add it to your order?" she asks.

"Ha, no. My husband recently bought one for his mistress. I found the receipt," I say, ever so nonchalantly.

"Seriously? That's messed up," she says, her face morphing back to annoyance.

"Yes, it is," I say as I take my long-ass receipt and walk away.

I hear the cashier say, "Take care," but I keep walking. My face is flushed with embarrassment, and my inner voice is cussing at me for even bringing up the Plan B. *"What is wrong with you?"* I repeat in my head.

What's wrong with me? I'm sick from sadness and betrayal. I'm worn down from single parenting and forgetting my medication. I'm brimming with envy when I see other people with responsible partners. I'm sick of this being my life.

I help Jude into his car seat and buckle him in.

"I love you, Mommy," Jude quietly says while touching my face.

Then, with tears streaming down my face, I say, "I love you," and give him a big smooch.

I shut his door, and before I get into the car to drive, I stop and look up at the sky.

"Thank you. Thank you for giving me my boy. Thank you. I'll be okay."

A new wave of emotions floods over me, but this time, it's filled with calm, peace, and gratitude. In this moment, I know that I will be okay.

11/12/22

UNCUT TRUTHS

"When deeds speak, words are nothing" ~ *Pierre-Joseph Proudhon*

Scrolling through Instagram, hoping to distract myself from the loop of court proceedings circling in my head, I come across a clip of Julia Fox, actress, model, and clothing designer, on the "notskinnybutnotfat" handle. With bleached eyebrows and no makeup, I watch as Julia says:

> "Just so you guys know, aging is fully in. Like, fully. Dirty girl. Ugly. Not wearing clothes that fit your body type, just fully wearing anything you want. All those things are in, and I'm suing if I see another product that says anti-aging on the label. I'm going to sue. I'm going to sue because I am going to age regardless of if I put that fucking $500 serum on my face. You all fucking know it and we know it so let's stop lying to ourselves. Getting old is fucking hot. It is sexy. It's probably the sexiest time in life, actually. Being pretty and hot in your 20s is the fucking trenches, and I'm not going back there."

My mind rewinds instantly to the first time my husband ever seriously scared me—it was April 11th, 2020, the night we watched *Uncut Gems*, starring, you guessed it, Julia Fox. It was also the night of our son's 2nd birthday, the same week he was diagnosed with autism. My husband had always hated holidays or birthdays, calling them nothing more than corporate money grabs. While I didn't necessarily disagree with him, I still loved the feeling of celebration, the feeling of being a kid again.

Aside from corporate greed, these holidays would always seem to trigger memories from Tripp's childhood that he didn't want to revisit. On this particular night, I expected some kind of isolation or withdrawal from him, as that had become the usual pattern. But tonight was different. His behavior was off, and his speech was slurred. I thought maybe he'd gotten super high—I didn't realize he was drunk, sinking into a darker side of himself that I didn't recognize. We had shared over eight years together, and I had never seen him like this. It was the first time he was fully blackout drunk.

There's a scene in *Uncut Gems* where Adam Sandler hides in his coat closet, watching Julia Fox's character, his mistress, undress without her knowledge. Julia's amazing body was hot; her natural, plump ass was definitely eye-catching. My husband began to get turned on by Julia, grabbing my hand to rub his penis over his pants. He squeezed my wrist hard as I tried to pull my hand away. His aggressiveness was not typical, nor attractive. He became forceful, and when I resisted, he got angry. I wouldn't have minded getting playful, inspired by a steamy scene in the movie, but this was different. I couldn't see any life behind his eyes.

I felt afraid. He ignored my firm voice telling him to stop—a request he would usually respect on the first mention. But this wasn't my husband; his face, his voice, his movements were foreign to me. His strength made me fearful. I got away from him and crawled into my son's crib, holding my child tightly because I feared what might happen next.

I wedged Jude's back into my chest in a spooning position,

knowing I wouldn't let this child leave my body without me. A few minutes later, I heard Tripp walk up to the crib. I shut my eyes, pretending to sleep. I began to pray in my mind: *"God, Universe, Source, grandpa, my angels, whatever is there, whatever is real, please, please protect us. Please protect us. Please shield us. Make him go. Make him leave us alone."* I envisioned being surrounded by warriors, beings whose energy alone would shield and repel him away from us.

I could feel Tripp staring us down from above. I could smell the alcohol on his breath. After a few minutes that felt like hours, he stepped away from the crib and walked into the other room. I slowly opened one eye to make sure I heard his footsteps correctly. He was gone.

"Thank you, thank you, thank you," I prayed in my head to whatever could hear me.

THE NEXT DAY, my husband had scrapes and burn marks on his body; he couldn't recall how they got there. I found some of his clothes on the back porch when I woke up to let our dog out. Confused, I started walking around the house, ultimately discovering him naked on the couch in the living room.

I remember being struck with disbelief as I tossed out the kitchen plates I found broken in the bathroom sink. I leaned over the trash can, observing how one dish had broken into five even pieces. Each piece seemed to hold a letter of the word "trust."

In that moment, I didn't expect *Uncut Gems* to be a foreshadowing of my days to come. I couldn't have predicted that my husband would become like Adam Sandler's character—a man with another woman, while having a wife and kids at home. I didn't expect my husband to become an addict. And while it wasn't gambling, the hunger for addiction was just as palpable.

I was upset and in shock. He apologized profusely, acknowledging how unacceptable and fucked up his behavior was. He followed up with all the right words, vowing never to repeat it, promising to make it right. I believed him—because why wouldn't I? After tears and a long talk, I put on a good face for the family and my son.

My husband convinced me to drive to a little town where we had dreamed of buying a home. We found an empty lot that overlooked the water and let our son run around, as I tried to remain hopeful about the future. I categorized that night as a one-time issue that would never happen again. It felt safer to view it as a one-off, rather than see it for what it actually was—the inciting incident.

There's a picture I posted from that day on Instagram—of a picture-perfect young family, celebrating their child's 2nd birthday. No one would ever know what happened because I had already erased it from my mind, blocking it from my memory...until now, while I watch Julia go off about aging.

EVEN THOUGH I wholeheartedly agree with the message that aging is "fucking sexy," I find myself flooded with memories and feelings that feel dizzying. Julia Fox, the perceived catalyst for my husband's past behavior, speaks about how women are shamed into thinking they should strive to stay young and pretty so men will like them. She then categorizes pretty women in their 20s as being in the "fucking trenches." I couldn't agree more, and a wave of compassion for my husband's mistress washes over me.

The layers upon layers of fucked-up-ness of all of this coming together catches me off guard. So, to distract myself further, I decide to listen to Emrata's new podcast, *High/Low*, and the latest episode features a special guest... none other than Julia Fox.

"What am I meant to understand with these synchronicities?" I ask myself.

"What do I need to learn?" I ask the Universe as I press play.

"Sex for me has always been one-sided, but I think all women can say that. So if I don't really need anything from you, I don't see the point," Julia states.

"Truth and respect," I whisper to myself. Her thoughts on sex surprise me, and they don't align with how I've judged or imagined her to be. She had been in a public relationship with Kanye West, and I made assumptions about her that were not kind. I feel gross inside about how quickly I could dismiss another woman based on her dating history.

"I'm really desensitized to sex, too. It's just—it's not thrilling for me. I pretty much, in my teens, learned that I was a commodity, that I could get money or resources from men. So then it just became this game of, 'Okay, how do I become more desirable so I can get more money, and I can be like that bitch?' It's still them giving me the power. It's not my own power, you know? So it's a humiliating kind of position to be in, or humbling," she explains, labeling sex as a "trivial" act.

That same dizzying feeling from earlier reappears as I remember how my husband responded to seeing Julia's body on screen—how he eventually cheated with a 20-something. His mistress was willing to let him stay at her apartment for free while I believed he was sleeping at hotels as he worked on getting sober.

Pity runs through my veins for his mistress. Will she one day feel like Julia? Does she not understand that she is being treated as a commodity—a distraction, a body used for sex that enabled a man to run from his responsibilities? Maybe she enjoyed the sex and found fulfillment in the attention. Perhaps she views sex as a trivial act like Julia? Should I take a lesson from Julia and not give so much significance to their sexcapades? Instead, I could view it as insignificant. Just because I can't have sex without feelings doesn't mean my subjective experience should be projected onto other people. Maybe I'll never know or need to know, but I'm often distracted by the harmful nature of the interaction. Perhaps I'm analyzing this so in-depth because there's a part of me, deep down, that wants to excuse my husband's behavior, to change the narrative of betrayal. This would allow me to live in denial—or a fantasy—that ultimately does not exist.

I replay the part where Julia says, "Being pretty and hot in your 20s is the fucking trenches, and I'm not going back there." I laugh loudly at this seemingly over-the-top statement where she compares that time in a woman's life to being in warfare. But then I observe myself nodding while laughing, because it is true.

I've said more times than I can count that you couldn't pay me to relive my 20s. I don't want to be in my 20s, or look like I'm trying to be. I love how I finally know myself and understand my needs, and that I now insist upon them. That's a fucking freeing way of moving through the world. Tripp can have his woman in her 20s; I'd rather have my freedom and me.

11/13/22

"ACCIDENT"

"The worst a man can do to himself is to do injustice to others" ~ Henrik Ibsen

Julia Fox has since unlocked something in me. Wild to say, but ever since listening to her thoughts on aging and sex, my memories of Tripp, that night with *Uncut Gems*, and everything that followed have begun to resurface. And loudly.

They've appeared in my dreams—or what most people would call nightmares. Sometimes, a scene will flash in my mind. I've begun writing these memories down to understand how we recovered from that night and how we got to where I am now.

After that night, my husband mostly went back to being his usual self. He hadn't gotten blackout drunk again, and he didn't engage in binge drinking for many months. Occasionally, I'd notice the faint smell of alcohol on his breath, which he'd make light of, explaining that he'd just had one shot because, "Why not?" I felt concerned because I never saw him drink, and he started storing alcohol downstairs in his "man cave." Still, I assumed he had just the one shot he'd tell me about because things hadn't worsened. If anything, he appeared less anxious, more relaxed, and super silly with our son.

Tripp had always been told that he should do stand-up. He could make me laugh until I couldn't breathe, but things were slowly starting to shift. His humor became darker, almost sinister—and it was aimed at me. It was a natural progression, hard to pinpoint. It's like when a plant moves; you never see it happening because it's *so* subtle. One day, you walk in, and the plant is suddenly turned in a new direction, leaning toward the sunshine. That was Tripp, but he wasn't leaning toward the sun; he was leaning into darkness.

At first, the jokes stung, but I figured he was just letting some frustration out. I could take a jab or two. His twisted humor worsened closer to bedtime, after he'd had several shots, and it always served as an excuse for humiliating me. The only problem was, I wasn't supposed to be humiliated. It was "just a joke." If I objected, I was the problem: too sensitive, no longer fun.

I was aware that the dynamic between us had changed. I was a new mother, and I'd often, lovingly, explain things to him since I spent the most time with our son. I later realized that wasn't welcomed by him. Instead of expressing his feelings at the moment, his resentment would come out in strange ways.

One evening, during bath time, I saw the shift clearly. Tripp was kneeling by the tub, washing our son with Irish Spring soap. I gently suggested we use the liquid baby wash instead, explaining that bar soap might be too harsh for his skin. He laughed—too quickly—then said, "Here, catch!"

Before I could process his words, a urine-filled diaper hit me square in the face.

He laughed so hard, he couldn't breathe. Tears streamed down both our cheeks, but mine were from something else entirely. I stood there, stunned, while he gasped between laughs, promising, "I never thought it would actually hit you!" His great aim—the same one that made him a frisbee golf pro—had suddenly failed him, or so he claimed.

When I told him how mortified I felt, he wouldn't apologize. I was "too sensitive," and it was "just an accident." Even if it *was* an accident, didn't that deserve an apology? I tried to explain that our son had seen it happen, that it wasn't a good example for him, but Tripp just rolled his eyes. I was "reaching."

I spent so much time wondering what was wrong with me. Maybe having a child made me too sensitive? Maybe I had lost my fun side and was always looking for the worst in him? In hindsight, I realize this was a tactic to trivialize my feelings and needs, whether conscious or not.

Looking back, it's clear that Tripp's resentment toward me was a direct result of his past. I was no fun. I was the bad guy. I was the constant reminder that he couldn't do anything right. I was his mother. And, as such, he would treat me like his mother—the mother who left him sometime between 18 months and three years old. The mother he had to beg to let him move in with her and her new husband at 13, after his father had gone off the rails. From my understanding, she wasn't the warmest; she was emotionally neglectful.

So when he would get angry and emboldened—or even violent—he saw me as his mother once more, telling him what to do and reminding him that he wasn't good enough. But here's the thing: he wasn't a kid, and I wasn't his mother. He was a 6'4" autonomous man, who chronically dumped his years of trauma—meant for her—entirely onto me.

11/13/22

THE TRENCHES

"If you want to make enemies, try to change something" ~ Woodrow Wilson

I log onto my computer to insert some pop culture trash into my brain and see a headline about the Julia Fox "backlash" the day after her online rant on aging.

"Wait, what backlash?" I say out loud to myself.

I click on the link and quickly discover that, supposedly, older women are upset that Fox was talking about aging being "sexy," when she is only 32.

"Wait, older women??" I am so confused. I pause and think about how lucky I am to be in a profession where people respect me more as I age. In contrast, Julia is in an industry that casts women as grandmothers around 25.

Julia hit a nerve, exposing how divisive aging can be. I assumed the younger generation would be the ones to have something to say about it, but no. It's older women who feel that she has never experienced age discrimination or the challenges of a 50-year-old slowly becoming invisible in society. With each wrinkle gained, they feel as though their importance withers further. I catch a glimpse of myself shaking my head unknowingly. I stop and wonder why I'm annoyed with the older women for their judgment. I shouldn't be, because they have more life experience than I do, but I am. Shouldn't they want the younger generations to start being vocal about this and change the way we view aging? Doesn't that mean it shifts how men will see us? Maybe they won't search for the younger version of us?

I repeat again to myself, "Maybe they won't search for the younger version of us?" Eww. I feel so grossed out that this thought even crossed my mind. In my warped brain, I, for a second, envisioned a world where having a young woman to cheat with wouldn't be a perceived accomplishment—and that my value would stand firm with every passing year.

The 20s are the fucking trenches, even though society crowns them as the time when women look their most desirable. Something is wrong if everything else is shit in your life *but* your youthful skin. It is a privilege to age. Think about the alternative... it's fucking death. So why do we want to go back? Is it because we've been left for the young? Or is it about irrelevance—being overlooked? Do the wrinkles and gray hair scare me? Or do they scare the men who can't handle the reflection of time passing? Is their discomfort with aging projected onto us? Is that why women are expected to fight this invisible war with serums, injections, and Instagram filters, while men are praised for their salt-and-pepper hair and "rugged" good looks?

And why is aging always framed as a battle we're supposed to win? Each generation picks up the sword where the last one left it, carrying the weight of progress forward. But what is the cost of fighting to stay visible, to stay valued, in a world that so often tells us our worth diminishes with time?

Maybe it's not just about youth or beauty. Maybe it's about power. Because when we age, we gain wisdom, and with wisdom comes a quiet, unshakeable strength. And maybe that terrifies them —the idea that we might stop needing their validation altogether. So they redirect their fear, packaging it as our insecurity, hoping we'll stay too busy chasing youth to realize we don't need their approval anymore.

But I see it now. The fear. The game. The impossible standard. And maybe that's the real privilege of aging—the clarity to call it out and opt out of it entirely, to climb out of the trenches. Because we keep waiting for the day when it will feel easy, effortless, when the world will finally say, "You've done enough, take a seat, and let us honor you." But that day doesn't come. Not for Julia Fox, not for the women who feel unseen, and not for me.

Part VI

"Sight is a faculty; seeing is an art" ~ George Perkins March

11/15/22

TRUST THY MOTHER

"The hand that rocks the cradle is the hand that rules the world" ~ William Ross Wallace

I stand in the doorway, watching my parents pack up to head back to Ohio. They had come to stay for a week to support me during my virtual court appearance. After the last in-person court appearance left me emotionally and physically wiped out, I asked for help in case a similar thing happened. Thankfully, it didn't.

I can tell my mom doesn't want to leave, but my dad is itching to get back. My dad is a man of routine, and hanging around my house for a week during my lowest hasn't exactly been enjoyable. In contrast, an opportunity to purge junk, rearrange furniture, and transform spaces has made my mom come alive. I love how she came in and transformed the house with so much enthusiasm, surprising me almost hourly with her changes while I lay despondent in bed. She loves any kind of project around the house, and every item I gave her permission to discard—whether by trash or shattering—was met with excitement.

In fact, my mom brought me back to life by utilizing her unique trick to release pain: break things. We chucked several glass vases at a concrete wall behind the garage. Watching the vases explode was thrilling—a true release. We'd comment on which vase made the best shatter sound, laughing till our cheeks hurt. There's something really therapeutic about watching something associated with a hard time shatter into a million pieces... much like my life.

It isn't the best time for my parents to leave because I'm about to see my husband interact with our son on FaceTime for the first time in almost four months. I reassure my parents that I'm fine, of course, and that I'll be okay no matter what. Though my mother looks uneasy and reminds me, "Keep it about Jude. It's about Jude."

I shoo her away, saying, "I know, I know."

My mom can always sense when I'm getting soft. Now is no different, given that she's watched my optimism grow time and time again after getting the slightest bit of attention from Tripp, only to be let down when alcohol and drugs have inevitably been prioritized over our family once more. If I'm honest with myself, I'd acknowledge the fantasizing I've been doing—and I *despise* it. I keep letting my mind wander into a pool of hope, imagining how his sobriety will magically make him dedicated to working for our family.

I have visions of our family reuniting in person—kissing and hugging each other, then walking back into our home for good, united, together, stronger than ever. It's like when Kevin McCallister watches his whole family return after reuniting with his mother in *Home Alone*. Even though so much destruction and chaos ensued, it was pieced back together as if no time had passed... *sigh*. But that was a movie. One that I actually like to watch. And while I have felt like I've been living in a film during moments of dissociation, I don't have anything near a happy ending.

I'm not exactly sure where this blind optimism has come from. If I were to guess, it's likely those very movies I watched growing up. They gave me an unrealistic view of people. I've had every reason not to believe in people and their ability to change. Still, for some reason, I always believe some intervention or life event can and will suddenly turn on the light bulb in someone's head. While that light is starting to dim, it's still there.

11/15/22

SORRY

"Those who cry the loudest are not always the ones who are hurt the most" ~ Aesop

"I'm so sorry. I can't believe things have gotten so bad. I'm so sorry it took all of this to get me to stop drinking," he says to me, tears running down his face. All the right words are coming out of his mouth—the words I had prepared myself to wait years to hear, or perhaps never hear at all. I begin to sob, looking at him. It feels like my husband's soul, his personhood, is back in his body. I'm not sure if that's totally true, *but I want it to be.* I have yearned for it. The dark circles under his eyes, so prominent during his addiction, are gone. And while he's still puffy, his skin is a normal hue, no longer the malnourished tint from before.

Although our son isn't that interested in the call, I am. I stay on longer than I should, grateful to have some connection after so much silence.

After the call, I feel hopeful, very much in a fantasy land, which I weave in and out of. I negotiate the level of betrayal, wondering how much I should really be upset with him. I think that if it was just the alcohol, if he hadn't cheated, we could repair and maybe even be back together. My mind races around the cheating, not the financial abandonment or the endangerment to our child, which I'm ashamed to admit. I pace and consider calling him, knowing I shouldn't, because we're not supposed to be in contact outside of FaceTime with Jude. In this moment, when I feel that urge, I know I'm supposed to call a friend or distract myself for 15 minutes until the urge passes, but I just want to talk. My mother's words, "Keep it about Jude," ring in my ears. I know she's right, but she doesn't understand this bond, this pull, that feels greater than gravity itself.

So, I call. No answer. I call again. His voice. The voice that feels like home...

This sensation, this imagined emotional attachment, is trauma bonding. And though I know about trauma bonding from a psychological perspective, I don't fully grasp the hidden power it holds. With one phone call, I enter the repeated cycle of abuse: the perceived kindness, the devaluation, and the reinforcement. I may have withheld from contact for almost four months, but just like an addiction, it only takes the right words to get me hooked right back in. There is an intimacy that we step back into as if nothing has changed. This is called "assurances of love," or what the kids these days call "love bombing." He truly says every word I have dreamed of, and the safety I felt with him in the past comes rushing back. If the relationship was all bad, it would be hard for this cycle to continue. But since his feelings of remorse play like music to my ears, I fall right back in... and hard.

"Talk tomorrow after I FaceTime with Jude?" he asks kindly.

"Yes," I reply without pause.

"Love you," Tripp says softly.

"Love you too," I say back.

The call ends, and hope floods my chest like helium, lifting me to a place where anything feels possible. It's intoxicating, this surge of possibility, as if I'm on the edge of being transported back to my old life—the one where my little family is whole, intact, and untouched by all the wreckage. I can almost see it, almost feel it, and it's so vivid that for a moment, I let myself believe it's real.

The next day, I happily skip to the phone when I hear the FaceTime call ringing. I prop up the phone for Jude and watch Tripp try—or maybe pretend to try—to pull Jude into connection. But there's no softness, no curiosity, no real effort to meet him where he is. And here I am, sitting just out of view, biting my tongue, torn between wanting to step in and fill the gap for Jude and wanting to encourage Tripp to be more engaging. The energy feels off, especially when Tripp asks if we can talk privately three minutes into the FaceTime. "*It must be something serious,*" I think to myself, concern rising inside me.

"So, I am really having a hard time paying my bills, and I wanted to see if there was any way I could split the child support into two payments or if it could be reduced?"

It feels like the wind has been knocked out of me. I can't even process the words. I stare at the screen, trying to decipher if he's serious or if this is some kind of cruel joke. The man who has spent months bulldozing through our lives with his chaos has the audacity to ask me to lessen his burden? I'm quiet, but inside, my mind is racing, colliding with itself.

I finally manage to respond. I remind him, calm but pointed, of his mistress, the hotels that weren't hotels, and his nights at her apartment while I was caring for our son.

"She didn't mean anything to me," he says, as if this is supposed to soften the blow—as if the meaninglessness of it all absolves him. Then he mentions her contacting him first, how she somehow got his number from someone on set.

My anger sharpens. "Even if that's true," I say, cutting through his excuses, "you made her feel comfortable enough to write you. You must have flirted before the season ended, at the end of April, for her to reach out to you during the summer. And no one made you respond."

There's a hollow silence after my words, the kind that makes you realize the truth has just hung itself in the air, undeniable and ugly. I'm stunned, not just by his request, but by the sheer comfort with which he makes it—like he's convinced himself that asking this of me is reasonable, fair even. And for a moment, I marvel at the chasm between us, at how differently we must experience the world to have landed here.

"So, why'd you stay there? If you didn't have feelings for her. You were just using her? Another female to avoid responsibility?" I ask, my voice sharper than I intend.

Silence. He doesn't like my clarity—it's too bright, too exposing.

He avoids my questions entirely, pivoting instead. "What if I move back in for a month? If you still want a divorce by the end of it, then I'll agree to it."

And there it is. The delusion. But I've been delusional too. What did I think would happen by even engaging in this conversation? That he'd suddenly morph into someone different? He still wants everything on his terms. I feel so naïve and gullible. Of course, he thought he could use his words to get back in.

I make it clear that I don't want to be married, never again. I want the slate wiped clean. No matter what. This doesn't suffice for him. Instead, he tries another tactic. He attempts to persuade me with the promise that he will snuggle with me every night. Heat overtakes my body. *Consumed.*

The constant need I had asked for every night for over a year. Even though I am quiet in response (or lack thereof), he then confesses that the massive amount of Adderall he took would have likely made it impossible for him to lay down with me at night.

And then the next words come out of my mouth—that my husband didn't lie next to me for over a year and that I still stayed; that I didn't value myself enough to put my foot down; that it disgusts me.

And then, finally, I let him know that I now realize that my ask—or my need—was not a huge ask of a husband. That I've already learned that a man will hold you... and will do so happily, without strings attached.

Oops. I said it.

"What? Who have you been with?" he demands.

"I haven't slept with anyone. I asked a man to just hold me, and he did, and that's truly all that happened," I share, as I am internally kicking myself for letting this slip.

"You had a man in the house?" he asks.

"No. I went to his house, and we literally spooned on the couch. And that's it."

He begins to cry. I start to feel bad for him. But I also feel angry that he thinks it's appropriate to even question me like this. Intense regret fills my body, and I get off the phone.

Then, the pattern continues.

He calls incessantly. I'm not strong enough to block him, so I finally answer.

"Hello," I say.

Silence.

"Please speak. This is what you used to do, and it's weird and manipulative. It's not cool to just call and then be silent."

"Why'd you have to tell me that?" he asks slowly, in a low, sad yet angry voice.

"What? About being held?" I ask, shocked again that he's turning this on me.

"Why'd you have to tell me that? You knew that'd crush me," he responds.

The epiphany. This is the pattern to make me feel guilty. He's blame-shifting. Another abuse tactic.

"Wait, you want me to feel bad for you when I found a Plan B receipt after you were lying to me about staying in hotels when you were actually staying at a girl's apartment and fucking her? Are you kidding me?" I state firmly. "I went and sought attention because of your actions. Do you think I actually wanted to be with a different person? I was forced to move on because you cheated and still wouldn't get sober."

"Why'd you have to tell me that?" he says again.

I hang up. The chaos has begun. Fuck. Why the fuck did I think we could be different? Why did I even talk to him!? I'm so angry with myself. He hasn't changed.

He calls again. And again. Shit.

The texts start.

"So, you can call me the other night, but I can't call you?"

Shit, why did I call him in that weak moment? I'm so stupid!!

"Stop calling. We've gotten off track. The focus needs to be on Jude, not our marriage. We have to do what's best for him, and I'm sorry I didn't keep my composure last night. Focus on your sobriety, I'll focus on my healing, then we will focus on Jude."

He shifts his approach next with, "I'm sorry for giving you a hard time about that guy. If we don't talk, I feel like I'll lose you."

"Nothing can be fixed in this moment. Just focus on yourself, and I'll see you tomorrow on the FaceTime, okay?" I reply.

He agrees, and the texts stop.

The weight of my mother's advice crashes down on me. The words, *"keep it about Jude,"* echo in my mind like a mantra I failed to repeat. I can see my mother's face as she said those words, her jaw tight, her eyes locked on mine with a fierceness only a mother protecting her daughter can muster. The image makes me cringe, my stomach twisting into knots. She was trying to anchor me, and I floated away. I'm filled with guilt about calling him, for leaning into the fantasy of him being back from the dead, for trauma bonding with a beast.

The next day, he FaceTimes for four minutes with Jude, then we hang up. Later that night, he begins to obsessively call. He texts me to "please call him back." I don't.

In the past, I would have felt so badly for ignoring his calls, but I do not have to do anything that does not serve me. I have to focus on supporting my mental health.

I wake up the next day, and everything is okay; the world didn't end. I walked right up to the ledge, but instead of continuing down into the abyss of abuse and codependency, I turned around and walked away, choosing my own peace. The gratitude for my life and circumstances overwhelms me. I will protect this peace like nobody's business.

11/15/22

TRUST THY FRIEND

> *"There is a place that you are to fill and no one else can fill, something you are to do, which no one else can do."* ~ Florence Scovel Shinn

"I mean, it's more narcissistic abuse than domestic violence," I say, trying to downplay what happened at the end of my marriage. I'm out to lunch with Vivienne—Viv for short, a former colleague and friend. We met while working at a college counseling center, and she's the kind of person you admire instantly—crazy smart, no-nonsense, and a little intimidating. Of course, Viv also specializes in domestic violence, which makes me feel even more exposed as I recount the last few months of my life.

"But isn't narcissistic abuse also domestic violence?" she says, though it sounds less like a question and more like a matter-of-fact statement. I pause, thinking. Yes, I know both are forms of abuse, but they don't feel the same. Abuse comes in all forms—emotional, physical, sexual, financial—but for some reason, I still can't bring myself to call what happened *domestic violence*. The word just feels too harsh in my ears.

"Yes, I guess they are the same," I admit. Viv doesn't seem convinced.

"Narcissistic abuse is a specific type of domestic violence, or in this case, intimate partner violence (IPV)," she says before taking another bite of her sandwich.

"Why is it IPV now?" I ask.

She holds up a finger, signaling, "Give me a sec," while she chews. After swallowing and taking a sip of her ice water, she explains.

"Well, ya know, domestic violence can happen with a parent, a sibling, roommates. People needed to understand that it's not just about marital partners. It got so stigmatized in that way, like people only associated DV with couples, but it's more common and complex than that," she says.

I feel embarrassment rising inside.

"Saying IPV specifies that the violence is between partners, whether or not they live in the same household," she continues.

I feel myself growing annoyed, wanting the topic to change. It's like I'm back in grad school and am not a professional with a private practice. Viv can see the shift in my energy—just from the look in my eyes and the way my body tenses.

"Mere, I'm not saying this to school you, I'm legit concerned that you don't realize the severity of what you've been through. No matter what label we put on it, it was violence with a hefty dose of coercive control," she says, shaking her head as she sets down her sandwich and wipes her fingers.

"My head feels foggy. Explain coercive control for me," I say.

"Depriving you of the means to escape, keeping you from independence, stripping you of autonomy," she states. I still don't fully grasp what she means in the context of my situation. She can tell that I'm skeptical, like I can't quite piece it together in my mind.

"Remember when you'd doubt yourself, question your own reality when Jude would get sick because of his comments? That's coercive control. Spending your money—coercive control.

Checking your phone, listening to your conversations—coercive control..."

"Okay, I get the point," I interrupt. "Look, I hear you, but this is making me sick. All those scenes are playing in my head, and they're ones I want to forget," I say, cutting her off.

"I understand. I just can't have you minimizing all this. I wouldn't be a good friend if I let you. Victims are usually empathetic, like you, and that amazing quality is exactly what made you attractive to him. Your kindness could be twisted, molded into something that made you overlook all the horrible things he did. And you want to see the good in people, of course, you don't want to believe that he could harm you. And so, slowly, you'll start to remember the good times, believe his sob story, his childhood trauma, his deflection, and convince yourself that it wasn't as bad as it really was... and the cycle continues." Viv says.

I snap back, "I'm not going to get back with him." I feel insulted that she'd even imply it.

"I know you aren't, but you'll be dealing with him for the rest of your life. You share a child, and he'll use any opportunity to continue this form of abuse. It always ramps up when the victim walks away. The co-parenting situation you're hoping for? It's likely not going to happen. You'll need to stay strong, far beyond the time this wretched divorce ends," she says. Her seriousness takes me by surprise.

"All the ways he was able to get to you before, he'll try them again. Especially with a child. That will become his new form of control," she adds.

"Well, that's the wrong area because my claws come out when it comes to Jude," I snap.

"But don't forget the slow and covert ways he manipulates. It may not be as obvious as kicking a gate at you, but there will be tears, gifts, words—anything to pull you back in," she warns. I know she's not saying this unless she knows I need to hear it. I feel the weight of her love in her words, and for the first time, I let my guard down.

My chin drops, and tears fall onto my lunch. She grips my hand.

"I'm scared. I'm really scared that I'll never escape this nightmare," I say, my voice cracking, the lump in my throat making it hard to breathe.

"You will. I promise you. You will," she says, looking at me with such certainty that I can't help but feel immense comfort. I nod and wipe my eyes with a napkin, dabbing at the cat eyeliner that's starting to run.

"You will become a fighter. You'll realize you didn't deserve any of this. Once you get past this stage of shock and denial, the anger will rise, and it will never let him control you again," she says with a fire I've never seen in her before.

I think she sees more in me than I see in myself, and at the same time, her words bring me relief. It's a quiet relief—like a weight lifting, just a little. Her belief in me feels like an anchor, pulling me out of the fog. But it's also terrifying. It means I can't pretend anymore.

"You can do this. You can face this," she says again. My tears come, but they don't feel like weakness this time. She reaches across the table and squeezes my hand.

"I can do this," I whisper, almost to myself.

"Yes, you can," she states, convicted.

"I can," I say while keeping my eyes locked with hers. The words don't come out with conviction—not yet—but they're there. And that's something.

11/18/22

GLIMMER

"Simplicity is the final achievement" ~ Frederic Chopin

"Could life be this simple and calm?" I wonder as I soak in the crisp morning air, the sounds of birdsong weaving through the quiet. My eyes wander over my backyard—a humble 5 x 20-foot strip of grass, more like a patch than a yard. The frost is slowly creeping in, but somehow, everything is still thriving.

My jaw clenches, and pain spreads across my chest; my mind turns dark with fear, signaling that there is danger. *"Did I forget something? I shouldn't be letting myself relax because there's likely something I should be doing, right?"* I ask myself.

No, there's nothing. There's only peace. And it feels so fucking goooood. I remind my body and mind that I am safe and I'm allowed to have this time to myself. I am still getting used to this new life.

"It makes sense that you're feeling on edge. You're unsure of what life will look like next," says my friend and mentor, Tim, validating my feelings and reassuring me that I'm not crazy.

I find myself nodding in agreement because I really do have a blank picture of my future, probably for the first time since I can remember. There's always been something to work toward—school, a job, a living situation to figure out—and then a refocus on something "better." I've always been so focused on building a life, considering someone else's perspective, and holding it in higher regard than my own.

"You don't have to know what it looks like," he reassures me.

"But that's kind of scary. I have no idea what to do. I'm having to reimagine myself and how I fit into this world completely," I reply.

"That's okay. Focus on finding your peace and what you like," Tim says, while I begin to let some tears fall. It sounds too simple. Could it possibly be that simple?

An hour later, when my mind and body start to shake in fear, I say, "Keep it simple, Mere." I look around, seeing bills on the table, a messy house that needs to be cleaned, my husband's books on the shelf, the lack of food in the cupboards; it's all so overwhelming.

"What is simple?" I repeat to myself again. "Follow that." I'm genuinely unsure.

My garden. I almost run back to the beautiful flowers and plants out back. I adjust my chair and just stare at them for a while. Is this what my life could look like? Could my mornings be peaceful, with a few days filled with my clients, and the rest available for rest? Art? Or writing? What if my current reality, which feels like I'm wrapped in a warm, cozy weighted blanket, could be my everyday? Could I feel protected to experience peace daily like this?

"I deserve that," I say out loud, surprising myself with the confidence in my words. I'm not sure if it's my friends' and family's incredible support, my angels and ancestors, my Higher Self, or all of it combined, but in this moment, I begin to believe it.

Christmas 2022

"The best apology is changed behavior." ~ Unknown

I am at home in Ohio, four days before Christmas, my favorite holiday. My son is super sick, and in a weak moment, I call Tripp, worried about our son. During the call, I ask how he is spending Christmas. And he tells me that he is now staying at his mistress' apartment over the three weeks he is off work, while she is supposedly out of town. The words crush my eardrum.

In the bathroom, I lean over the sink, trying to calm myself after taking in such obliterative information. I look up at myself in the mirror and into my own eyes. They look different. Not better, not worse, just different. There are more spots in the iris now. I stop and watch the whites of my eyes turn from a milky hue to fire. Anger toward myself fills me once again. Anger that I didn't predict this. Anger that I fit perfectly into a cliché. Anger that I fucking care.

"I expected more from you," I say with vengeance, looking into my own eyes. If the "old me" had a portal to peek into and see the current state of my life, she wouldn't have believed it. The destruction is too great.

Memories invade my mind, and one in particular plays from when I first met Tripp. He had just ended a long-distance relationship and couldn't commit yet. I appreciated his honesty and remember watching him explain while he sat at his desk. I sat on his bed, and after nodding, he got up and walked toward me, kissing me out of nowhere. It was sensual and invigorating.

After our kiss, he hesitated to begin again.

"What's wrong?" I asked, confused by his apprehension.

"I just feel like I'm doing something wrong, like I'm cheating," he replied.

Maybe he was. Maybe he was cheating with me because, a month later, he met up with his "ex" in Costa Rica to see if they could make it work.

More memories begin swirling in my mind, and I feel alone because I don't have him anymore.

"Stop!" I yell at myself.

I walk out of the bathroom and back to my childhood bedroom. Knowing I need a distraction, I pull out some of my scrapbooks from under my bed.

There I am as a child. Strawberry blonde hair crimped in a side pony with bangs. My fair skin dotted with freckles, an abundance of them. My grandpa would say they were the marks of angel kisses. Kids at school would say they were from a cow that pooped on me. Regardless of the stories, I liked myself back then. I wasn't exposed to the world's cruelty—or at least, I didn't understand it. I love that little girl, and she still lives in me. She is happy without makeup. She has hooded eyes that don't need to be masterfully concealed with a cat-eye. She has spaces between her teeth that braces would eventually fix. Still, she is smiling easily, unlike the closed-lip smiles I currently wear to hide my teeth.

I am transported back to my 8th birthday, the smell of bread baking at Pizza Hut filling my senses. I look down and see the maroon carpeting beneath my feet. It feels like a dream, sitting squished in an overcrowded booth with my friends from school. There are balloons and smiles as I scan the room filled with people—they are all here just for me. My mother is attentive to all the details, still, I know inside she is likely anxious; she always gets more impatient when she has to host something.

My mother is beautiful. She has jet-black hair, the kindest eyes, an infectious laugh, and a killer figure, except she doesn't think so. Since I can remember, my mother has been on a diet and believes in always wearing makeup before walking out the front door. She is often adjusting her clothing to make herself look "thinner," likely due to her own mother's demeaning comments and her brothers' critiques.

One time, when my grandparents were having a family cookout, my mom arrived with a beautiful cake to share. I witnessed my mother's tears and consoled her in the car after my grandmother opened the door and asked, "Why would you bring a cake to our house when you know you shouldn't be eating that?"

Looking back, I'm proud of my mother for turning around and leaving, but it was hard when my words of endearment, "Mom, you are so beautiful," didn't make any difference to her.

My mom is generous and kind, always putting people in front of herself. So when I lock eyes with her, I know I am safe because she is always solid and stable.

I scan the room and realize that my father hasn't arrived yet. I know that he is likely at the golf course. I was so proud of him because my father was an excellent athlete and a star basketball player in high school. He would have been a professional baseball player had he had some guidance from his father. I know this because I've heard him say this many times. My dad always turns angry or frustrated when his father is mentioned. At this point in my life, I don't understand why, but I sense it's not good.

So Pizza Hut. Growing up in southeastern Ohio, having a party at Pizza Hut is a big deal. At my party, it feels like I am a full-blown teenager and can chat with my friends at a real restaurant, something I have been dying to do up until now. After finishing the pizza and breadsticks, hyped up on soft drinks, my dad finally arrives, and all eyes turn to him. He makes a big entrance.

"There's my birthday girl! I made a hole-in-one today. Can you believe it?" he shouts, grinning, while he explains that he only had to hit the ball once for it to go in the hole.

"Wow," I say proudly, only half understanding what he means.

"But I made it to your party. I might have played my personal best, but I'm here," my father says.

"You did that for me? Oh, you didn't have to," I repeat because I have heard my mother say that. I feel badly inside, like I ruined my dad's chance to have a new personal best.

I remember looking around, and recognizing that my friends Maggie and Kourtney were watching our interaction. Maggie's dad was never around, and her stepdad, Danny, was really more like her father, even though she didn't call him that. Then I looked at my friend Kourtney. We knew things were off in her house because we'd sneak down the steps to the basement to spy on her dad. We could always hear some loud noises, even with the door shut. We often heard strange moaning as we crept open the door. I once bent my head in and saw a naked body on the big screen TV he had installed behind his pool table. I heard the clang of his beer as it sat on the glass table. I knew whatever was going on wasn't right, so I grabbed Kourtney's hand and we slowly inched our way back up the steps. Her father would soon leave Kourtney, her sister, her brother, and their mom, and never reach out on her birthday.

I always wondered how Kourtney and Maggie felt about my dad being at the party. I felt special because he was there; that it meant I was special. I internalized the idea that I should feel lucky or grateful if a man/father stops what they are doing for me. It's so innocent in retrospect, but I think it was the beginning of continuous messaging from society to myself and my young female friends that we're lucky if a man/father showed up for us, especially if they were doing something more important than a Pizza Hut party, like getting a hole-in-one.

Part V

"It is better to act and repent than not to act and regret" ~
Niccolo Machiavelli

03/2/23

BLACKBIRD

"In the small matters trust the mind, in the large ones, the heart" ~ Sigmund Freud

Heading south on Highway 9, the air feels lighter, like a quiet promise of change. The buds on the trees hint at spring, and the warmth makes me bold enough to roll down the windows. The wind tangles my hair as I turn up the music, letting it fill the car and push everything else out. But the present moment can't hold me—my mind drifts back to last night, pulling me into the memory. I spent the night with a younger man—a farmer.

I'm driving, but I'm not entirely here—I'm back with him. There's dirt under his nails from working in the soil every day. He doesn't move away when I touch them, inspecting the beauty of his creases, the grooves in his skin from the daily work he puts them through. Those hands wrapped around mine all throughout the night, our bodies intertwining with ease and familiarity, like we'd done this a thousand times before, even though we hadn't.

The whole evening plays out in my mind, start to finish. We spent it braiding rope for his necklace, our hands brushing now and then. Later, I nestled against his bare chest. He read me poetry, his poetry. I listened, taking in the moment, but I struggled to focus. Not because of his gorgeous face or the tone of his voice—it was the genuineness, the way he shared heart-filled words and then met my eyes to check in.

He spoke about the gifts from the earth and about light and dark. I felt a pool of tears gather in my eyes. A drop fell down the crease of my nose, sitting there as if it were observing too. "Little tear, you are lucky," I thought to myself, "You are lucky to bear witness with me."

When he finished a section of his poetry, I looked down and said, "I'm sorry, but this is making me emotional." It was my way of warning him, letting him know I might cry—expecting, on some level, that he'd stop reading.

Instead, he said, "I'm honored it makes you emotional. It should make you emotional," then continued on.

What was this foreign experience I was having with this man? Was he actually real? Aside from my shock at his comfort with emotions and vulnerability, I was struck by the level of intimacy this creature was sharing with me after only being around me a total of four times.

Driving home, the memory of him lingers, warm and glowing, until it's suddenly eclipsed by a sharper, crueler memory. It hits like a sucker punch, and I begin to weep.

I cry for the version of me who was so neglected, who didn't believe this kind of connection was possible.

I cry for the fear that kept me stuck in complacency, terrified of being alone.

I cry in horror that I lived through such emotional isolation.

I cry in gratitude that a light to the other side was shown.

I cry in honor of this experience, for I can't "unknow" what I now know.

I hold these complex feelings all at once and then, without thinking, I begin to softly sing: "*Blackbird singing in the dead of night, take these broken wings and learn to fly...*"

The words slip from my mouth, unbidden but perfect.

I pause, taking in the lyrics and my surroundings.

"Mary. You are here. I love you. Thank you."

"Blackbird" was Mary's favorite song, the song that her 14-year-old daughter sang at her funeral.

I instinctively know Mary wanted this for me. She played a part in connecting me with this young man, even though it was only for a short while. The farmer served a distinct and needed purpose: a glimmer of hope that I can experience gentleness from a man.

Mary longed to be a writer and to be free from her marriage, just like me. She wouldn't have these goals realized in her lifetime, but I would. Sometimes, I think she's writing through me, like these words could be hers right now and we are sharing in each moment, whether in a man's arms or writing words on a page.

Mary was a successful psychiatrist who specialized in substance abuse. We were connected by a shared client, but quickly went from colleagues to friends. She helped my private practice prosper by refusing to send me clients until I increased my rate, insisting that I honor my worth.

After disclosing my marriage issues with her, which I felt had been impacting my ability to handle the severity of a shared client, Mary listened quietly but made non-judgmental utterances of, "mhmm" that signaled I was safe to share.

Before her death, we would take walks around the dog park and discuss our marriages. It was shocking at times how eerily similar our husbands were, and the similar dynamics bonded us. She would encourage me to break the cycle, sharing her regret about not leaving. She expressed how painful it was to be stuck in a marriage at the end of her life, knowing that she never gave herself the chance to know something different.

She stated that if she did not have metastatic breast cancer, she would have left; that she deserved to know freedom from daily covert abuse. It was hard to hear that his abuse increased after the diagnosis. It's like he knew he would never be found out and got daily pleasure from pressuring her to have threesomes and making her feel small. She had almost no hair, constant yeast infections from chemo, and difficulty walking, yet this man continued to treat her this way. He is lucky that I only met him briefly before I knew this information.

Mary knew she was going to die within a matter of months. Listening to her reflections on her life right before death was powerful. It gave me a sharp awareness of time and an urgent push to critically evaluate my decisions. I vowed to think of her every time my heart got soft.

Aside from relationship discussions, we'd talk about Mary's fear of death, how she didn't believe in the afterlife, and how scared she was to become "nothing." Mary knew I was spiritual and disagreed. I'd often say, "But no one really knows. What if there is something else after death? Don't hold so tightly to your belief that there's nothing. What does that even do for you? Why not just let your imagination go wild?" Mary would just smirk, but I knew I was making her think because she began referring to me as her "death doula."

Being a so-called "death doula" wasn't exactly new for me. During my mid-20s, I became extremely close with my work colleague Joyce; she was in her late 60s and became sort of a mother figure to me. She was diagnosed with lung cancer years after surviving breast cancer. She believed she'd survive cancer a second time, and I was her cheerleader and friend, covering shifts when she was at chemo so she wouldn't need to take a vacation day after using up her sick days. I was there, providing emotional support, until I couldn't anymore. She died on August 30, 2012.

With Mary, I would encourage her to think about the ways she could give her children and friends messages if life beyond death was real. We talked about the possible signs she'd send to signal to them that she's safe. I was met with a side-eye, but I said, "C'mon! Just indulge me!" Eventually, she began to imagine.

"I think I'd send a blackbird," she said.

"Oh really? Why is that?"

"I love The Beatles song 'Blackbird,'" she said. "You should hear Rebecca play it on the guitar. She's incredible."

"I love that," I replied. "So, where would you like to die?"

"I'd love to be in the warmth, on a beach in Florida."

"Ok, let's get you to Florida!" I replied.

"I can't. I don't want to die up in an airplane. I'll have to die here, with the kids," she explained, and I nodded.

I'M about an hour from home when a car with Florida plates cuts me off. I laugh to myself, shaking my head. Florida. The state is a mess of contradictions, much like the memory it conjures. Suddenly, I'm back there, on a beach during the holidays of 2022, the salty breeze tangling my hair, grief heavy in my chest.

I had flown to Florida for two reasons: to honor Mary and to save a marriage that, in hindsight, I should have let die long before. It was Mary who consumed my thoughts as I walked the beach alone, barefoot in the sand, the waves rolling in their endless rhythm. Mary, who had died just weeks before, surrounded by her three kids and husband.

I stopped at the water's edge and wrote her name in the sand, a simple offering. *Mary*. The tide crept in, gently washing the letters away as I whispered, "I love you." I stood there for a long time, staring out into the horizon, feeling both hollow and full at once.

And then, as grief often does, it shifted into something more mundane: hunger. My stomach growled, so I turned back toward the hotel, seeking distraction in food.

What happened next has stayed with me in a way that felt surreal then and feels no less so now.

I sank into a random beach chair by the pool, letting out a sigh as I scanned for a waiter to take my order. That's when I spotted him—my husband—stationed at the bar, slowly sipping from a rocks glass, his posture too casual, his focus elsewhere. "Can't be alone for a second without trouble," I muttered under my breath, shaking my head.

He must have felt my gaze slicing through the distance because he turned, startled to see me there. As he made his way toward me, a big, glossy blackbird swooped down, cutting through the air with effortless grace. It flew right past his head, landing just inches from me, its presence impossible to ignore—majestic, grounded, and demanding attention.

"Wow," my husband shouted, "look at that bird!"

I turned to observe it—a striking blackbird, maybe a raven, perched confidently next to me. It stayed there as I ate, unbothered by the curious stares of people passing by, who couldn't help but do a double-take at the unusual sight of such a large bird calmly keeping me company.

"It's Mary," I said softly, more to myself than to him. "She told me she'd come back as a blackbird to let me know she was okay."

"Pfft," he scoffed, rolling his eyes with the kind of dismissiveness that always made my skin crawl. "Whatever you say."

As soon as the words left his mouth, the bird let out three deep, resonant calls—echoing, deliberate, almost as if they were meant to silence his doubt. Then, just as gracefully as it arrived, it took off into the sky.

I smiled, my heart swelling. I didn't need him to believe. I knew.

AS I PULL into my driveway and put the car in park, my phone buzzes on the passenger seat. I pick it up, expecting a text from my mom or maybe a follow-up from the farmer, but instead, it's an unfamiliar number. I open the message, and my stomach clenches. It's from Mary's husband.

"I think it is really messed up that you said you'd stay in contact with Mary's family and you didn't. Don't make promises you can't keep."

Wow. Just like that, I'm yanked back into the aftermath of her death, to the strange and heavy space he dragged me into after she passed.

Before Mary died, I gave her children my number and email, along with letters to each of them. But to my surprise, it wasn't one of her kids who reached out first—it was him. He wanted to have lunch, said he needed to be around people who knew Mary.

Deep in my bones, I felt a nudge that said, "No." I knew I shouldn't meet with him, and since I was finally done ignoring my own instincts for the sake of other people's feelings, I told him I'd reach out in a few weeks. I was dealing with my own personal mess —trying to hold myself together while my marriage crumbled—and I just couldn't do it.

The night after his request for lunch, guilt started to creep in. I found myself pacing the house, wrestling with the idea of refusing him. Finally, I lit a candle and spoke out loud to Mary.

"Mary, I don't think you'd want me to meet with him. I still feel guilty, though. Can you give me a sign that I'm right?"

The flame, which had been flickering, suddenly stilled. And just like that, I felt still too, filled with peace for the first time in weeks.

But now, staring at this text, the peace feels so far away. His words—aggressive, manipulative—confirm what I already knew. I'd only promised to stay in contact with her children, never him. I knew the way he'd treated her, and frankly, I was surprised he didn't think she'd told me.

Still, I responded with as much grace as I could muster.

"I know you're grieving, so I'm going to ignore your accusations. I'm going through a divorce—something Mary supported me in pursuing. I don't have the bandwidth to meet."

I knew he could feel the ice in my reply. He sent back a long, overdone apology, but I didn't bother replying. As I read his message, I saw Mary's face in my mind, laughing—a kind of vindication that told me she agreed.

4/28/23

PRISONER

"Bad company ruins good morals" ~ The Apostle Paul

It's been about a month since my night with the farmer—a month of trying to hold onto the sense of peace I felt in his presence. But life has other plans, and peace doesn't come easy when you're unraveling from a marriage that refuses to let go.

I'm standing in my kitchen, my suitcase still half-unpacked from last week's women's retreat in Grenada. The trip feels like a distant memory, even though it was only days ago. Grenada was supposed to be a reset, a breath of fresh air, a reminder that I'm more than this divorce. And for a few days, it worked.

Now, I'm back, and reality has reared its ugly head in the form of an email notification.

The first email arrives:

"ConEd is no longer in my name and will be turned off by the end of the day. Call them before midnight to avoid shutoff and have the account put into your name."

Then another:

"I will be doing the same thing with car insurance for your vehicle."

Frantically, I forward the emails to Celeste, my lawyer, hoping she can help me navigate this. My bank account is currently overdrawn. Quickly, she coaches me on how to respond. So I do:

"You have to maintain the financial status quo since the forms haven't been signed. I will let the court know."

While anxiety fills up my insides, I press send. I fear how he will respond and if this is enough to convince him not to act on whatever he's angry about in the moment. I know he doesn't want the divorce, but I do. I feel like he's punishing me for divorcing him. He wants me to hurt, but does not see that when he hurts me, he is ultimately hurting our son.

Five minutes later, his response:

"Cool. How was Grenada?"

"Grenada? How did he know about Grenada??" I keep repeating to myself. I don't need to justify why I was there, but I am going to anyway. I felt like I was going to die. I needed a break from parenting, from life, from responsibilities, and I needed help. I needed sisterhood, I needed my friends. I needed to be reminded that I am more than this circumstance and that my life won't always be this way.

My friend Malaika is from Grenada, and if you read *Hey Addiction*, you know how I met her and why I needed her. She was also going through a divorce with an addict while being a full-time mama. I knew I'd be safe with her; things would be understood without saying a word. I had to go. Tripp had begun canceling the supervised visitations with our son more often, and since he was living with his "girlfriend" without responsibilities, I felt I deserved a little retreat. I was desperate. As such, I put the whole cost of the retreat on my credit card. It was financially irresponsible, but I did not care.

At the same time, I didn't want him to know where I was, and it was none of his business; there was a protective order in place. I didn't post on public social media, and I was confident that the people who knew I went kept it private.

Dread overcomes me. I look around the room, feeling as if I'm being spied on. My mind spins as I search each corner for a recording device. I know, on the surface, this may sound paranoid and strange, but let me provide some context. My husband works in the entertainment business, specifically with sound. He would often place devices all over the house when he began drinking. When it was his time to "parent," back when our son was little, and I needed to run errands—whether to grocery shop or take a walk—he'd pop on his headphones, believing that putting a listening device in the room would suffice. Then, there were times when he would interrupt my phone conversations to defend himself. At first, I was confused, but I would soon realize that he was listening in with a strategically placed wireless recorder. Even as I write this, I'm realizing just how strange it was. I would justify it as a safety precaution for our son, but now, I see it for what it really was—a form of control.

I spend the next several hours scouring the apartment, looking in every nook and cranny for a wireless recorder. I grab a trash bag and begin discarding anything and everything that reminds me of him. Eventually, I give in to the realization that I won't be able to find any device, and I'll have to be extremely careful in my own home. This causes me to shake; my legs and teeth begin to involuntarily tremble. My body knows I'm not safe. *I feel trapped.*

"HE MUST HAVE HACKED into your email," Maria said after I frantically called her, hoping she hadn't spilled the beans.

"No, there has to be someone spying for him," I reply, my voice shaky.

"Check your password," Maria insisted.

I have three emails—one for work, one personal, and one for my side business. Following her suggestion, I check my personal email, and sure enough, I had "signed on" in North Carolina, where Tripp is visiting his parents. There had been multiple logins over the past two days.

How could I have dismissed Maria again? How could I have forgotten to change my password and set up two-step verification? What else of mine has he read?

The feeling of violation crashes over me, familiar—like the night of *Uncut Gems*.

Turning off the electricity was revenge. I'm not allowed to have a life if he can't be with me.

"I'm in prison," I whisper to myself, as black spots cloud my vision.

5/12/23

NEW SUPPORT

"A very little key will open a very heavy door." ~ Charles Dickens

"They were asking for me? The plant medicine?" I ask, surprised and confused.

"Yes, they kept repeating your name. They said that you are already in tune with them," James replies, his words full of conviction. "I had to let you know."

I'm sitting across from my dear friend Elara and her husband James, trying to process what I'm hearing. After what he refers to as the "dark night of the soul," James began a spiritual journey—one that is almost entirely in contrast to the life he lived before. I can't speak for him, but I believe one of his greatest shifts came from his experience with Ayahuasca, the plant medicine that was calling for me.

I've known about Ayahuasca for a long time, intrigued by its transformative effects, but I've never actively sought it out. I've always been fascinated by the intersection of science and nature, particularly how ancient tribes understood how to utilize certain plants for medicinal purposes. They knew something on a deeper level—something modern society often struggles to comprehend.

From what I've learned (forgive me if I don't describe this perfectly—always do your own research), Ayahuasca is a sacred psychoactive brew used by Indigenous cultures in the Amazon for spiritual ceremonies and healing.

The ingredients are simple: bark and vine. But not just any bark or vine. It's specifically the Banisteriopsis caapi vine and the leaves of the Psychotria viridis shrub. These plants grow only in the dense jungle and take years to mature.

I've long been fascinated by near-death experiences (NDEs) and how the chemical DMT is released both at birth and at death. This is part of the reason NDEs occur.

I explain to James that I've done some research on Ayahuasca, but I can't experience it since I'm on Zoloft, an SSRI (selective serotonin reuptake inhibitor). Ayahuasca is known to release serotonin, and since my medication already increases serotonin in my bloodstream, my health could be at risk. Surprisingly, too much serotonin can be harmful. I'm stunned by the high dose I'm on, especially because of the divorce. I know my psychiatrist doesn't want me to consider lowering it until sometime after the divorce is over. I share these disappointing realities with James.

Thankfully, he has another gem to offer me: Evangeline deArmas.

During his time at the Ayahuasca ceremony, James met Evangeline. He speaks so highly of her, explaining the progress he's made with her. But he's quick to add that she's not a "typical therapist."

"What do you mean?" I ask, curious as a therapist myself.

He explains that she combines family systems therapy, somatic work, spiritual guidance, and reiki.

"Okay, I'm open to it. Feel free to give her my email," I say, ready to embrace whatever help I can get.

THAT EVENING, James introduces Evangeline and me through email. From there, I begin my research into her background and titles—more like *titles*: integrative counselor, psycho-spiritual guide, and shamanic practitioner.

I'm open. I've seen a serious transformation in my friend, and I know I need the same. It also feels good to be cared for. James and Elara knew what I needed before I did. Lately, I've had trouble leaving my home and pulling myself out of the loop I constantly help so many others escape.

Financially, I'm not in a good place, and it feels foolish to pay $250 per session a week for 12 weeks. Yet, there's a feeling inside me that it would be worth it—that I must connect with her, at least for the free 30-minute consultation. With the divorce dragging on and legal bills stacking up, what does a little more debt matter? This is an investment, and I know I need the help.

I jump on the Zoom consultation and am immediately met with one of the most beautiful human beings I've ever seen. Full, curly, voluminous hair—almost a dark version of Keri Russell's hair from season one of *Felicity*. Glowing skin, high cheekbones, and the most intense eyes—they hold a depth of wisdom that feels almost piercing. Eye contact with her feels electric. She feels both ancient and young, radiating calming vibes that I can feel through the screen. I can't place her into any specific category of human. You know what I mean? We, as humans, judge based on first impressions. This time, I can't, and that's both exciting and intimidating.

We connect immediately, realizing we speak the same language. We both approach our work with clients holistically, but she goes further. She openly discusses spirituality and focuses on somatic work. While I weave in aspects of spirituality with clients who are open to it, I've never felt as confident about how essential this aspect is to healing and transformation. She is a true integrative counselor.

I share everything that has happened to me, including my financial insecurities, depression, nightmares, body pain, fatigue, and lack of appetite. She has a lot to take on, but I never once feel like I'm too much for her. It's a relief. I'm ready to start a new path of healing with her help.

5/15/23

"PICK ME" BULLSHIT

"Life is as tedious as a twice-told tale" ~ William Shakespeare

I've heard that anyone of significance who enters your life becomes a teacher of sorts while on this Earth. In my mind, the farmer could be my guide, though I hoped he'd be my teacher of pleasure. I could feel the Universe chuckling, knowing I was trying to control the plan.

I started traveling upstate occasionally to visit him. His busy farm and summer landscaping jobs limited our time together, but I welcomed this distance. I was actively seeking a casual connection without serious attachments. He was intentionally different from my ex. The farmer values spiritual relationships and prides himself on transparency—qualities Tripp lacked. Early on, over ancestral animal-themed tarot cards, we discussed our past relationship wounds. He yearns to be a father, which contrasts with my fear of pregnancy. I no longer have fallopian tubes, and yet I know I never want to mother another child. Nothing between us is hidden; he knows my situation and desires, yet I still hold onto hope, despite knowing our time together has a clear expiration date.

One evening, seated at his kitchen table satisfying our munchies, I expected a simple snack, but watched, mesmerized, as he skillfully prepared gourmet guacamole from fresh vegetables. His focus and skill unexpectedly intrigued me, revealing a new side I found oddly attractive.

Our conversations invariably turned deep and meaningful, exploring why we found ourselves single at this stage of life. We shared openly about our roles in past relationship breakdowns, fostering vulnerability and trust.

"Tell me about a time when a problem surprised you by being a problem for the other person, something you didn't initially see as an issue?" he proposed, his knife rhythmically slicing a carrot.

Reflecting briefly, I chose a safer example from my marriage, downplaying its complexities.

"During the pandemic, we had this shift in the relationship because I began to make more money, and he oddly became sort of jealous. I mean, it was during the pandemic and my work was in high demand," I explained. "The jealousy was surprising; he was out of work for almost seven months. It wasn't really that hard to make more than someone else if they aren't working," I said with a laugh.

The farmer seemed tense, perhaps missing the irony in my anecdote. There was a pregnant pause before he asked, avoiding eye contact, "Is it important for your partner to earn more money than you?"

"No," I answered hastily, a blatant lie. The truth was woven into the small details I'd picked up on—the modest apartment, the careful comments about money, the way his work ebbed and flowed with the seasons. It was clear he lived with the constant pressure to stretch what he had through the long winter months. I didn't want to bruise his pride, so I played along, but in doing so, I betrayed my own truth. Internally, I scolded myself for slipping into old habits—

the ones where I pretended to be more easygoing than I really am. *You're still trying to be the cool girl, making others comfortable,* I silently rebuked myself.

SHE—MY inner voice—was right. Why did I lie? Financial stability is my non-negotiable. It's the hard line I draw in the sand, a survival instinct born from being exploited financially by my ex and clawing my way through single motherhood. But there I was, betraying myself in real-time. For what? A few more warm nights in his arms? I could see where this was heading, and yet, I hesitated. I hesitated to trust my own damn instincts. Instead, I was trying to figure out how to fit myself into his life, as if that could ever work. But deep down, I knew I was grasping at something that was never mine to hold.

I felt the familiar tug-of-war between my ideals and my reality. I didn't want to be seen as superficial, the kind of woman who judges a man by the thickness of his wallet. I pride myself on valuing character over currency, connection over convenience. But the truth, the uncomfortable truth, was that I also crave security—the financial stability that has eluded me for so long. The thought of stepping back into that struggle with someone else made my chest tighten. I want someone who can stand beside me as an equal, someone whose life isn't built on such shaky ground. Yet admitting that felt like a betrayal of the person I want to believe I am. I could feel the tension between who I aspired to be and what I needed to feel safe, and I wasn't sure how to reconcile the two.

The irony isn't lost on me: my own relationship with money is far from perfect. Who am I to pass judgment? I pride myself on being fiercely independent, running my private practice and making it work on my own. But since having a child to fully support, I've been stretched thin. The resentment toward my ex for his lack of financial foresight has grown, but so has the resentment toward myself—for not choosing someone more stable, for not seeing the signs sooner.

Deep down, a darker thought lurks: *Would anyone truly successful want me?* It is a belief rooted in the cracks of my self-esteem, and it isn't pretty. It was that night that I realized the farmer had become my teacher, showing me exactly where my wounds are still raw. But clearing out the rot is my job, and it's going to take more than a little pruning. It's going to be one deliberate, painful step at a time.

9/12/23

SURRENDER

"The greatness of a man's power is the measure of his surrender" ~ William Booth

I crack open my window, letting the crisp autumn air fill my room as I prepare for my session with Evangeline. My notebook, already open, catches my eye with a message highlighted in bright green ink:

"You must pull the arrow back to launch yourself forward."

These words glare at me. I don't know where I heard the saying, but I wrote it down for my clients to reassure them that taking time for themselves isn't a step backward—that moving backward is an illusion distracting them from their best interests. But now, the message hits too close to home. I feel like I might throw up, knowing it's time to move on.

This realization has been churning deep within me, reverberating through every part of my being. I can't ignore it any longer: I can't make it work in NYC anymore.

So far, the divorce has cost me $33,000. With little cash on hand, I've had to spread it across credit cards. To secure my lawyer, I paid

$15,000 for a retainer. That was used up with all the court hearings, and within a few short months, I had to pay another $15,000. My credit card minimums are through the roof. My YouTube channel is barely breaking even. Mentally, I can't take on more clients in my private practice; I don't have the emotional capacity, and I can't afford the childcare to do it. Babysitters in NYC cost a minimum of $25/hr. Tripp has stopped paying child support, and I know I'll have to take him to court for that. Friends are randomly giving me things they no longer use—like a Sonos speaker or high-end clothes to sell. I am thinner than ever, and I need support. I need my family. I need to be home.

Ohio hasn't always been good to me, but every time I've lived in Columbus, I've thrived. My son is only a few weeks into kindergarten, and I know disrupting his schedule won't be good for him. He's autistic and thrives on routine.

"You have to think about what's important for you, too. He needs a healthy and happy mama. That matters just as much as his need for consistency. You'll be able to give him that and more. He will be around his grandparents, aunt, and people who love him. This is not black and white. This is not you choosing yourself over your child; this is very much choosing what your child needs most—a healthy mama," my therapist affirms, validating my feelings.

Relief, guilt, and shame mix together in my body, and streams of tears fall down my face. I have to leave it all behind. I feel like I don't have a choice but to go. I don't know when Tripp's going to sign the divorce papers, when he'll face his addictions, or when he'll financially support us again. Everything is unknown. Except that it's time to go.

"DOES IT HAVE A DISHWASHER? I need a dishwasher," I ask my parents as they show me the first apartment in Columbus over Face-

Time. I'm trying to get a sense of my options if and when I move back.

"It does!" my mom says enthusiastically. "And Mere, look! It even has a fenced-in backyard!" She's thrilled that I'm even considering moving back to Ohio. She didn't think she'd see the day.

"Wow," I whisper to myself, suddenly picturing my son running in the grass, laughing.

There's a part of me that feels like I'm doing something wrong, like I'm taking our son away from his father. I have to keep checking this feeling with reality. We're living in the same city as his father, and he isn't making an effort to get sober or see his son. Deep down, I fear that if we leave, he won't make an effort to be in our son's life at all.

I pause to acknowledge my fear and remind myself that it isn't a reason not to act. It's there for a reason, even if I don't know what that reason is right now. I decide to write to it.

"Hi fear, it's Mere. You're here again. I welcome you. Even though you make me uncomfortable, I know you're still valid. I hear you. I see you."

My therapist has talked about welcoming every emotion, as each one serves a purpose and has value. Instead of letting fear overtake me or stuffing it down, I'm going to acknowledge its presence. When I do, the overwhelming feeling starts to fade.

Part VI

"I am no child, no babe" ~ Shakespeare

10/13/23

FRIDAY THE 13TH

"The world is beautiful, but has a disease called man" ~ Friedrich Nietzsche

It's Friday the 13th of October 2023, a day long labeled "unlucky." Which is ridiculous, considering 13 is Taylor Swift's favorite number. Shouldn't that alone invalidate the superstition? But no—13 still gets the short end of the stick, thanks to centuries of patriarchal nonsense. In elevators, it's as if the missing 13th floor screams, *"Screw you, witch!"*

I remind myself that 13 is, in fact, sacred: the number of lunar cycles, the number of times our bodies align with the moon each year. Once upon a time, Friday the 13th celebrated the divine feminine in all of us—men included. Somewhere along the way, the Middle Ages happened, and instead of revering women, we were vilified. Goddesses became demons. Women became witches. And anger became crazy.

My phone pings, interrupting my musings. It's Elara:

"I'm listening to Julia Fox's book when I'm bored of pregnancy books, and it's actually really good! You may like it 😭"

Julia Fox strikes again. The woman who inexplicably stirred my husband's desires during a moment of intoxication, forcing me to escape from his clutches. Wait. Why did I just phrase it that way? The connotation is that Julia is at fault, not my husband. That her body was the sinful catalyst that made him act out of character. By wording it this way, I unconsciously perpetuate the notion that she is responsible, rather than holding my husband accountable. Despite believing I am enlightened to the realities of patriarchy, its deep-seated influence clearly still holds me captive.

Driven by curiosity, I promptly download her memoir, *Down the Drain*, on Audible and slip on my headphones. I anticipate a brief listening session, but hours pass as I become completely engrossed. Julia's candor, unfiltered and exposed, captivates me. She fearlessly confronts the darkness within herself and the forces that took advantage of her vulnerability.

One story in particular jolts me: Julia hears buzzing from the bathroom and finds her partner trimming his pubic hair. In that instant, she knows he's cheating. And yet, she doesn't confront him. She doesn't have the energy. She's an exhausted mother, burdened with a drug-addicted partner who consistently fails to meet the bare minimum of supportive parenting.

I freeze. Suddenly, I'm back in July, standing outside a bathroom door. My husband was visiting for lunch—our son, my mom, and I all gathered at the table. He'd gone to shower first, and I remember waiting forever for him to finish. When I finally knocked and entered to use the toilet, he was manscaped to perfection, hastily drying off.

"That's odd," I thought at the time. But then Jude cried out, and I rushed away, forgetting all about it. Now, I realize it wasn't odd. It was a clue. One I missed.

Listening to Julia, I feel both admiration and shame. She let herself feel angry. I didn't. She didn't rationalize her partner's actions. I did. And when her husband demanded his passport for a trip, she handed it to him—with the first page torn out. I think, "She's so crazy," but then my hand slams down on the counter.

"Stop. Stop labeling her reaction," I tell myself. She wasn't crazy —she was *right*. She was *angry*. And she had *every right to be*.

Why can't I give myself that same grace? Why do I suppress my anger, judge it, hate it? Because I've been conditioned to see it as ugly. As "masculine." As not "feminine."

But anger isn't ugly. It's a signal, a boundary, a force for change. The patriarchy has convinced me that anger is a man's emotion, and I've swallowed that lie whole. For years, I've shoved it down, terrified of being "like my dad" or "too much." I never let it teach me. I never let it protect me.

And now, looking back, I see the price of that denial. My anger has been there all along, there to show me the truth—to reveal the lies, the betrayal, the disrespect. But I refused to listen. I shoved it aside, choosing peace over power, silence over strength.

No more. Julia's story reminds me that anger isn't the problem; it's the suppression of it that causes harm. Anger is not just a masculine force—it's a divine one. It's Kali, the goddess of destruction and transformation. And it's time I learned to embrace her.

10/23/23

KALI

"If you find me not within you, you will never find me. For I have been with you, from the beginning of me" ~ Rumi

While I was in high school, I was surprisingly moved into the advanced English track, before AP classes existed, and we were assigned Shakespeare. Reading Shakespeare was both hard and easy for me. If I read line by line and translated it into modern language, I'd have the hardest time. But if I listened to the dialogue in a section, I could feel what was being said and "translate" from there. My favorite was *The Taming of the Shrew*, mostly because of the movie *10 Things I Hate About You*, but I also loved *Macbeth* because of the quote, "By the pricking of my thumbs, something wicked this way comes." Is it a little strange that I enjoyed the witches? Maybe. More importantly, I knew the sentiment of that saying—they were talking about intuitive feelings. I connected intuitive feelings to the sensations in my body, yet forgot about this as I grew up.

This type of communication is backed by science but has been described colloquially with funny sayings like, "Your ears are burning" to indicate someone is speaking about you; "Shiver down the spine" to say danger is near; or "Were your bones aching?" to suggest a storm is approaching. "By the pricking of my thumbs"—even back in school, I knew it was the same. And for me, it was my anger.

As I move further and further out of the emotional abyss and onward with my new life, I begin experiencing my body for what feels like the first time. With Evangeline's help, I can identify where I'm experiencing physical tension in my body, learning how it connects to my emotions. Intellectually, I've always understood that most issues are psychosomatic; still, I've been far from prepared to address my anger.

I've always had a negative association with anger. If I had to guess, I'm sure it's due to my mother's discomfort with its expression. I've internalized the belief that anger indicates a failure to regulate emotions, a need for better articulation, or most commonly, that it's a precursor to violence. I have always been incredibly, if not annoyingly, bothered by violence. In the past, I would not watch or enjoy movies that contained violence, and at times, I wouldn't even let someone finish a story without interrupting and asking if it contained violence, usually because I could sense it was coming. Most of the time, I was right; my antenna for violence is always on alert.

Evangeline begins discussing how every emotion is valid and equally as important as the others. While I thought I already believed this, I quickly learn that I am judgmental about anger; I struggle to really believe it has purpose. I've finally made peace with envy, understanding that if I'm envious of something, it's because I desire it. I've been working on my relationship to fear, softly challenging it while also understanding it. But anger? I am not ready to face anger.

"I want you to write a letter as your anger toward yourself," she requests with ease.

"Um, what?" I reply.

"Imagine that your anger is a separate being. What do you think it wants you to know?" she asks, her voice light, as if this is some simple task.

Internally, a wave of frustration rises, and I feel that familiar knot of resistance tighten in my chest.

But I nod—because I always nod, don't I?—and pretend like I'm processing, like this isn't some huge, uncharted territory. I want to tell her I don't want to do this, but I can't. Instead, I feel a cold anger rising in me, the anger I can't seem to direct anywhere. It's not just about the request; it's about everything that led to this moment: the years of pretending I had it all under control, the numbness that's been my companion for so long. The idea of confronting this now, on a deeper level, makes me want to shut down, to walk away.

But I can't keep leaning into my old patterns. I know that therapy has been helping me tremendously so far; I know I have to stay open to the process.

I sit with myself, trying to understand how anger can be as valid and equal to happiness. What purpose does it serve?

Then a vision comes to me.

It's me, standing on the steps of middle school at 12 years old. I'm waiting for the bus to pull up, headphones on, blasting Fiona Apple's debut album *Tidal*. I love this album, especially the track "Sleep to Dream." The brooding drums give the feeling that a storm is imminent, while the lyrics speak truths that need to be heard—specifically by the fool who has done her wrong. Then the piano comes in, and it feels like she's hitting the keys with both skill and rage. She is underestimated, used, seen as a pawn, but she is saying—*no more.*

Fiona is speaking, and she will be heard. She is powerful. And she is angry. Anger. I do like singing angry songs, so I must like anger. I sit with that thought for a moment. Then I ask myself, "What did listening to that song and feeling those angry emotions do for me?" I ponder this

Anger signals to me that I've been wronged. It validates me. But then, and most importantly, it releases me. It all makes sense.

Then, anger writes me a letter:

Meredith,

I have loved you since the moment you were born. I have been waiting for you to acknowledge me. I am not bad. I am just as important as your other emotions. I will not hurt you. I will protect you. Please, don't stuff me down anymore. I will help you know whom to trust. I will help you generate the courage to act. When you begin to feel me, please become curious about my appearance. I am here to signal when it's enough. I am here to signal when to act. I am here to signal the truth. I will be here for you. Please use me.

My anger has been neglected. It is essential for me to move through emotion. I now recognize that when I honor my anger, I feel a release. I move through the emotion faster and then feel free of it.

During my therapy session the following week, Evangeline suggests that we explore my anger further. She encourages me to research the Hindu goddess Kali as "homework" for our next session. This is one of the many reasons I love Evangeline's approach—she recognizes that wisdom can be found in every religion, spiritual practice, ancient culture, or text, a belief I hold deeply, too. It's a stark contrast to how I was raised, where identifying with one religion meant rejecting all others.

After our session ends, I immediately Google Kali. Her image stops me in my tracks—blue skin, multiple arms brandishing weapons, and a tongue defiantly sticking out.

As an outsider who is not Hindu, I acknowledge that I am in the process of learning about Kali and do not claim to educate anyone on this. My exposure to this religion has been limited. However, I am in awe of this goddess and the rich spiritual tradition that surrounds her. Kali, it seems to me, represents the shadow self in all of us—a primal, wild force that we all possess, but often repress or ignore.

From what I've learned, Kali is often depicted as a fierce, wrathful figure with a sword in one hand and a severed head in the other. Kali is considered to be the goddess of death and destruction, but she is also seen as a powerful force that can bring about great change and transformation. Her destructive nature is not viewed negatively, but rather as a necessary aspect of creation and renewal. She is complex, representing destruction and darkness, but she is also seen as a protector and defender of the innocent. She is a symbol of strength and power and is often called upon by those seeking to overcome obstacles or break free from negative patterns of behavior.

This is why I was told to research Kali. At first, I was unsettled by her appearance—how could she, with blood dripping from her chin and skulls hanging from her limbs, be a protector of children? But then it clicked: because many things can exist at once. Protector and destroyer. Fierce and nurturing.

When I was in Grenada for the women's retreat, I was introduced to an album made up of mantra loops. One song repeated, "*I am a Warrior and I am a Healer.*" The more I listened to the pounding drums and the repetition of the words, the polarity began to make sense. Warrior and healer—two opposing forces somehow perfectly in sync.

Even now, I feel that fierce mama bear energy when it comes to my son. The instinct to protect him is primal. If anyone or anything dared to harm him, they'd have to face me—and I wouldn't hesitate. I wouldn't cower in shame if people knew I had hurt someone to defend him; I'd wear it like a badge of honor, standing tall with the predator's skull in my grasp.

Kali's anger is not chaos—it's protection, fierce and unwavering. It's love in its most feral form.

In Western society, women are rarely seen in their full complexity. There's an unspoken rule that we must keep our anger hidden, a constant pressure to be soft and gentle—especially as mothers. Meanwhile, the narrative casts fathers as the protectors. But what happens when the fathers aren't doing their job? And, more importantly, why can't both parents be protectors?

These questions linger in my mind, but I remind myself to focus on what I can control—my own relationship with anger. By honoring and embracing it, I tap into a primal energy that fuels transformation. Kali's duality—the power to destroy and create—reminds me that my anger, too, holds this potential. It's not something to fear or suppress but to respect as an essential part of my humanity. When I channel it with intention, it's not just a force within me—it's a force for positive change in my life and, by extension, the world.

Anger, I will not suppress you anymore. I love you.

Thank you.

10/30/23

NOLITE TE BASTARDES CARBORUNDORUM

"The sight of a coward's blood can never make a warrior tremble" ~ James F. Cooper

It's been almost a year, and I'm back in line at CVS to pick up my prescriptions. Luckily, it's a solo trip to the pharmacy this time.

Standing in the dreaded line of customers staring into the white light of their phones, I decide to fight the conditioning of these dreaded devices and resist following suit, especially since developing some carpal tunnel-like symptoms.

I look around, free from the hex of a screen, and instead am lured by the Halloween decorations on the shelves around me. There are stuffed toy spiders with fangs and plastic witches that cackle, startling unsuspecting customers as they walk by. I grin every time I watch someone flinch and even laugh out loud when a passerby stumbles, alarmed by the creepy sounds pulling them away from their devices. I glance down below the register, hit with the reminder of what real fright lurks beneath. Though this time I've been spared, there is no Plan B for sale in sight.

It's my turn. I walk up to the cashier, a beautiful young woman who should be in a magazine, not working at CVS. I, meanwhile, am incapable of just being normal; therefore, I must make fun of my purchase of Xanax.

"I have to be on these babies because of my divorce," I say with a smirk.

The cashier looks at me sweetly and says, "I'm sorry."

"No, no, don't feel badly for me, it's a good thing. I'm almost free," I say, hoping that this will soon be true, and to relieve myself of the awkward exchange I just unnecessarily created.

The cashier, with her kind eyes and perfectly curled black hair, begins to fidget, pulling at a crease in her sleeve a little and looking away from me while waiting for the psychiatrist to clear the order.

"*I've made her uncomfortable. Why can't I just keep my mouth shut? I don't have to joke about everything,*" I think to myself in embarrassment.

She then turns toward the screen and I see her eyes fill with tears. I look down, trying not to make this situation any more awkward when she whispers, "I think I'm about to be going through one too."

My mind immediately goes to disbelief as I begin guessing her age, assuming she's too young to have even been married. It's funny how I have a stereotype of what a divorcée would look like, especially because I'm almost one and never imagined it'd be me. My chest begins to ache with empathy, and I fight the urge to throw my legs over the counter to give her a long, hard hug.

"I promise, you'll get through it. It'll feel like you're dying, but you will survive." It is so bizarre being the one giving the encouragement.

She wipes a tear from her cheek, one that fell like a hard rain. She scans the room, checking to make sure her coworkers aren't observing her. When she realizes everyone is busy, she turns to me quietly.

"I have three children, the first one from a previous relationship, and I was so happy being a single mom. When he came along, he wanted children of his own, so I had two more. I caught him cheating, and now he's acting like I'm the one in the wrong. I don't know what is happening. He isn't helping me out with money, so now I have to work two jobs while my mom watches the kids. I feel like I'm in a nightmare." There is an intensity, a desperation in her voice, almost as if she's still trying to grasp her reality. I know this feeling deeply.

This feels like a scene from *The Handmaid's Tale,* us sharing our real names from "the time before," before our lives were savagely taken from us. Even though we've provided children and served the men, our outlook is grim as, inevitably, we will end up in the Colonies.

"Do you have a lawyer yet?" I ask.

"Not yet, but I'm getting one this week. Even though he's already moved in with the other woman, he's making up things about me, talking as if I'm a bad mom," she says as a tear hits the counter. "He must be a narcissist, right?"

At this moment, I'm triggered, yet I'm confident because I can speak from experience. I shake my head and roll my eyes.

"Does he drink or use drugs?" I ask, and she immediately nods.

"Ignore the threats, focus on yourself, stay the course. Let him bury himself because he will. Know your truth. The truth will prevail in the end. Ignore his abuse. They are just words, not truth. You're a good mom. Keep being a good mom, and be good to yourself. I promise, you will come out on the other side."

Just then, the psychiatrist approaches, and we quickly adjust our postures, acting like we weren't just having the most intense conversation about our shared experiences.

"Do you know this medication can make you feel drowsy?" the psychiatrist asks.

"Yes," I reply.

While he punches in some numbers, I rummage through my bag, pulling out my last business card. As he walks away, I slip it to her.

"If you need help navigating anything, contact me," I say, paying for my order.

She mouths "thank you," and I see a flicker of relief on her face. It doesn't mask the pain, but she knows she's not alone. She looks at the logo on my card, then slips it into her pocket.

I hear a man sigh loudly behind me, a clear sign of impatience. I turn my head to acknowledge the rude utterance. Of course, a rotund man with beady eyes is staring at me through his tiny glasses, sliding down his ski-slope of a nose. I shoot him a "fuck off" look before taking my receipt.

"You've got this," I say firmly as we lock eyes one last time.

11/1/23

CATWOMAN

"If I be waspish, best beware my sting" ~ *Shakespeare*

Clad in a full-body black latex suit, reminiscent of Michelle Pfeiffer's Catwoman, I perch on the roof of a house across the street. My home lies before me, shrouded in darkness. Like a guardian of the night, unseen by anyone, my eyes scan every detail, ready to thwart any potential threat. A heavy blanket of dark, ominous clouds hangs overhead, casting a foreboding atmosphere, punctuated by distant rumbles of thunder. My senses heighten, and a surge of adrenaline courses through my veins. If I catch even the faintest glimpse of him, I will pounce.

In the ethereal realm of dreams, I find myself deep in the woods, hidden among the trees. My gaze fixates on him as he leisurely smokes a joint, his attention captivated by the flickering flames of a small fire. Like a spectral apparition, I shift positions within the woods, effortlessly teleporting from one vantage point to another with a mere blink of my eye.

Behind him, a wicked smile curls upon my lips, and I lick them in a feral, predatory manner, anticipating the moment to corner my merciless prey. My Catwoman guise bears the scars and gashes inflicted upon it by him—my abuser. Before him, the cashier from CVS sits with a forlorn expression etched across her face. He looms over her, a towering menace. In this moment, I embody the fiery defiance of Ofglen from *The Handmaid's Tale*, primed to strike Aunt Lydia with a deadly blow.

With swift and calculated grace, I launch myself upon his back, my limbs elongating unnaturally as they bind his flailing arms. A cold shiver runs down my spine as my knife finds its mark, slashing with unrelenting fury across his throat. The rage consumes me, propelling me to continue the assault, driving the blade deep into his back, puncturing flesh again and again, until my breath falters and I collapse upon the ground, panting for release. My body drenched in sweat, I am satiated by the exhilarating power to take control, to protect not only myself but also the helpless cashier.

Moments later, I jolt awake, my body drenched in a chilling sweat. I peel the comforter away, my trembling limbs guiding me toward the bathroom. Gazing at my reflection in the mirror, a profound transformation is evident. My eyes, once familiar, now bear a darker intensity, their sharpness piercing through the shadows. Did I access Kali? I feel a resurgence of power coursing through me, a strength summoned from within, a reminder that I am not a mere victim, but a force to be reckoned with.

11/14/23

BURN

"We can't solve problems by using the same kind of thinking we used when we created them." ~ *Albert Einstein*

I'm in session with Evangeline, describing the relief I feel now that the fog of depression has momentarily lifted. I'm finally having more good days than bad, and I tell her how this shift feels like climbing to a new height after being stuck in a valley for so long.

"I'm starting to feel lighter," I say. "I think I'm finally letting go."

She nods, encouraging me to elaborate. That's when I remember a moment from the week before, when I was cleaning out my husband's things in the basement. I'd come across a black-and-white photo of him, taken on set at work. I'd loved it so much when I first saw it that I had it blown up. But there it was now, stuffed in a bag, forgotten and collecting dust.

"I didn't even hesitate," I tell her. "I just grabbed the photo and started ripping it up."

I describe how the soft, grainy texture of the paper felt between my fingers, how it crinkled and folded with each tear. At first, the pieces were large, and the tearing was quick and easy. But then I kept going, shredding it smaller and smaller until it was reduced to tiny bits. With each rip, something shifted inside me—like a weight lifting, a release I didn't even know I needed.

Evangeline listens intently, then asks, "What did that feel like for you?"

I pause, searching for the right words. "It felt...liberating," I finally say. "Like I was reclaiming something. It wasn't anger exactly—it was more like relief. Like I was letting go of who he was to me, piece by piece."

I sit with the memory as I speak, Evangeline's gentle gaze steady, encouraging me to go on.

"I wasn't just cleaning out the basement," I say. "I think I was looking for closure without realizing it. When I found that photo, it felt like it was daring me to hold onto something I was finally ready to let go of."

I recount how I took the remnants of the photo upstairs and outside with me. I placed them on a kitchen plate and lit a candle. "The wax dripped onto the pieces as the flame consumed them. I watched the black and white turn red, the crackling heat sending small embers into the air. It was oddly beautiful—like the photo was transforming into something else."

Evangeline nods, her silence encouraging me to keep going.

"When the fire sputtered out, I stood up, letting the remaining scraps fly into the wind. It felt like releasing everything he'd taken from me."

I pause, letting the memory settle before moving on. "The next morning, after I dropped Jude off at school, I walked by the garden. It was covered in frost, but I noticed a peachy-pink color out of the corner of my eye."

"My roses," I say aloud, recalling the moment. "I couldn't believe they'd survived the cold and wind."

I describe how I knelt down to smell the bloom, marveling at its resilience. "But then, right at the base of the bush, by the roots, I saw it—a shard of the photograph. Of course, it was his face. Perfectly intact, staring up at me."

I shake my head, the anger still fresh as I tell the story. "It was like he couldn't let me have one moment of peace. Rage just... took over. I grabbed the shard and shouted in my head, 'Haven't you stolen enough from me? This is my rose bush. This is my moment!'"

Evangeline raises an eyebrow as I continue. "I lit the shard on fire right there. Making sure I burned what was left of his face to ashes. I didn't feel sad—not even a little. I wanted it gone. I wanted him gone. When the ashes cooled, I blew them into the street. It felt final, like I was reclaiming my space."

She nods thoughtfully, her expression soft yet intentional. "That sounds freeing," she says, her tone inviting reflection. "What do you think has replaced the question, 'How could I not see?'"

I sit back, caught off guard. But then the words come easily. "I deserve better."

She smiles, placing her hand over her heart. "Yes," she says, her voice warm with affirmation. "You do."

I exhale, the truth of my words settling into my chest. "I deserved so much more," I add, my voice firmer. "I deserve peace. I deserve to move forward."

"It sounds like you've created the space to realize that," Evangeline says. "Your window of tolerance has expanded. You've cleared away what doesn't serve you, and now you're making room for what does."

I nod, her words resonating deeply. "Spaciousness," she repeats. "It's something you can claim right now. Between sessions, think about what spaciousness looks like for you—what you want and deserve to fill that space."

I leave the session with her words echoing in my mind. *Spaciousness*. He had consumed so much of my mental, emotional, and physical space. But now, I was clearing him out—piece by piece.

When I get home, I sit down with a notebook, pen in hand, and write the word "spaciousness" at the top of the page. Slowly, a list begins to form, each word pouring out as if I'm *finally* making room for all the things I have in store for myself.

<u>I can have what I deserve right now</u>

rest – quiet – babysitter – cook – calm – ease – writing – pondering – loving my boy – white – crisp – ease – water – windows – typewriter – time – plenty of time – write – sip tea – breathe for all I have – folded laundry – clean home – bright love – big home with New England feel – space from the pain – rearview – ocean waves washing it all away – relief – gratitude

11/28/23

CEREMONY

"I am larger, better than I thought; I did not know I held so much goodness." ~ Walt Whitman

"We are going to be hosting the next ceremony at our place with Evangeline," Elara informs me enthusiastically. It takes a moment for my mind to process this.

"Wait, Evangeline will be administering the medicine?" I ask, seeking clarification.

"Yes! Will you be able to come?" she asks. I'm caught off guard; I didn't think I would be included in this for some reason.

"I would love to, but I'm still on Zoloft," I reply. My psychiatrist has been insistent that medication is necessary.

"That's only for Ayahuasca; I'm pretty sure it's fine for psilocybin," says Elara.

"Hmm, I need to think and talk to Evangeline about it. I meet with her later today. I'm really afraid of it being painful. Both you and Remy had really physical experiences."

"I know, but it is worth it. You'll process so much," she says encouragingly. "It's a huge part of what prepared me for pregnancy," Elara adds. This statement carries weight, further cementing my consideration. Elara had been very hesitant about becoming a mother and really questioned if it was for her. There's a calmness around this subject now, leading to her ease during her pregnancy.

"I JUST HEARD from Elara about the psilocybin ceremony. Do you think I should do it?" I ask Evangeline at the beginning of our session.

"Absolutely," she replies simply.

"But what about my SSRI? I just can't feel the pain like Elara and Remy. I've had enough pain; I can't take more," I plead.

Evangeline takes in my concern and does an all-knowing Buddha-like nod.

"It is all about your intention," she says.

"But I don't even know what mine would be... Maybe to understand how to move forward?" I ask, clearly unsure of this process and what I actually need.

"What if your intention is to experience pleasure in your body?" Evangeline proposes.

"Pleasure in my body?" I'm really surprised that this would be my intention.

She nods again, all-knowingly.

I don't anticipate this intention, but she knows my experience—she understands how deeply I've been in a dissociated state. The only time I truly feel my breath or connect with my body is during our breathing exercises in session. I'm terrified to inhabit my body, where all my emotions are stored, because it hasn't felt safe. The pain of betrayal lives there, visceral and raw, much like being physically stabbed and whipped by his words. I do my best to explain to Evangeline that this intention probably won't work for me.

"The pain you've experienced in your body is exactly why you'd ask to know pleasure," she states.

I sit quietly, taking her words in.

"I do deserve that," I say softly.

She nods, validating my words.

"I don't think I can get childcare, and I'm on Zoloft," I say, challenging every angle before committing.

"I think you owe yourself this experience, and you have time to secure someone for childcare," she says. I nod in agreement. "The medicine may not have as strong an effect due to being on an SSRI, but it isn't prohibitive."

"You mean there's not the same risk as with Ayahuasca?" I ask.

"No, there's no risk of serotonin syndrome like with Ayahuasca," she says, continuing to explain more of the clinical implications between the various plant medicines.

"It does help that it'll be at Elara and James's. I love their space," I say, then pause for a moment. "Okay, I'll do it, but I'm nervous."

"That's okay, welcome all the feelings," she replies.

I begin to cry. It feels so new to be cared for, to be thought of, and to have someone encourage me to do something for myself in this way. I cry out of gratitude for the people who love me, especially when I'm struggling to love myself.

I STAND at the bottom of the steps to Elara's magical brownstone, unable to move. My legs feel heavy, like I'm stuck in place. There's a deep knowing that once I begin this journey, I will forever be different from the person I am right now. After several minutes of contemplation, I swear I feel a warm nudge at my side, gently urging me to take the first step up into their home. Nerves and excitement swirl in my stomach as I slowly gather my pillow, mat, and weighted blanket; I want to be prepared for anything, so I've brought every kind of comfort I could think of.

This home has always felt like a place of comfort, and as I make my way up to the entrance, my nerves begin to ease.

The heavy wooden doors creak as I push them open, and the rich, earthy scent of burning incense immediately fills the air. It's a sacred welcome, inviting me to leave the outside world behind. I step inside, and my eyes find her immediately—Evangeline.

This is the first time we're meeting in person, but as we embrace, it feels as though I'm hugging an ancient tree, solid and timeless. There's something grounding about her presence, as though the medicine we're about to share is already alive in us, humming in recognition of this moment.

Her voice is gentle yet assured as she offers words of encouragement. She gestures toward the room, inviting me to take my mat and pillow and find the spot that will be my home for the evening.

I make my way inside, weaving through clusters of people, instinctively drawn to the back. I settle into the same spot where, more than a year ago, I had slept on an air mattress after "the incident." As I unroll my mat, the memory creeps in—endless trips to the bathroom that night, my fingers scrolling through Google searches about Emily Ratajkowski being cheated on. It feels surreal to think about how I actually got to meet her not long after.

I sit for a moment, taking it all in. A smile tugs at the corners of my mouth. Life can be so strange. I shake my head lightly, marveling at the winding, unpredictable path that somehow led me here.

Carefully, I place my mat over the one provided, layering my energy onto it like a quiet declaration: this is my space, my moment. The scent of incense deepens, and I close my eyes for a beat, letting the surreal nature of it all settle in. The past may linger, but tonight, I am here. Fully here.

Before the ceremony begins, Evangeline explains her background, how she acquired the medicine, and expresses gratitude to everyone—from the Earth to our ancestors, to the North, South, East, and West. She reminds us that this is our personal journey and encourages us to not interrupt anyone else's. We are instructed to keep our blindfolds on, keeping the journey focused inward.

After receiving my chocolate dose, I fix my blindfold and settle into the sound bath.

I'm enjoying the soothing sounds when I hear it—James's loud, vocalized exhale from the other corner, and irritation surges through me. "*Oh, must be nice to be a man and just make sound at any volume,*" I think. I battle with myself inside my head. *Am I seriously going to be this irritable the whole time? You know, you can breathe out loudly too, Mere. Fuck, why do there have to be men at these things? Is my shit already coming up? What's my intention? She said to focus on my intention. Ok, pleasure in my body. This is not pleasurable; it's irritating my ears. Focus on the intention.*

I try to recenter, reminding myself to stay focused.

Then, just as I feel like I'm about to unravel, I hear her voice—Evangeline begins to sing.

It's strange, hearing your therapist's voice in a way you never have before. Her voice, powerful and divine, emanates from her body, and I can't help but be drawn into it. It takes everything in me not to take off my blindfold and start cheering. How could she have kept this entire side of herself hidden from her clients? Her voice is indescribable; all I know is that it's leading me deeper and deeper into my healing.

But my body, still tight with tension, resists. I can't find a comfortable position. I squirm on the mat, feeling the discomfort intensify. The music shifts, new sounds fill the room, and new sprays are being spritzed. One spray smells almost like cinnamon, and it comforts me, reminding me of something from childhood.

I move onto my hands and knees, finding my way into a cat/cow position, and then—*pop!* My stomach releases, and in an instant, I feel a *swoosh* as I'm pulled back into my body. It's like waking up. The knots in my stomach, which have built up over time, unravel in a single second.

I place my hand on my belly, feeling it hang for the first time—

it's a strange yet liberating sensation. I literally hold my stomach, afraid it might hit the floor. In that moment, I feel an overwhelming clarity. Some kind of trauma has released, and I know this shift is a pivotal part of my healing.

I lower my head into Child's Pose, feeling my stomach gently press against my thighs. As I breathe in, I notice something new—air filling my stomach completely, a sensation I've never experienced before. I can actually take full breaths. Every moment is like the first time.

I let myself savor these deep breaths, letting my chest rise and fall with a rhythm that feels ancient and steady. As I exhale, my back sinks into the mat beneath me, releasing tightness I didn't even know I was holding. The warmth of the sun pours over me, not just kissing my skin, but enveloping me, as if the universe is tucking me in for the first time in years.

I raise one arm behind my head—the arm that has long refused to cooperate, stiff with the weight of years of stress and overuse.

Even with my blindfold on, I feel a shift. The ground beneath me softens. My mat disappears, replaced by warm grains of sand that mold to my body. The scent of salt fills the air, and the distant crash of waves reaches me. My rational mind wants to argue, to pull me back to the room I know I'm still physically in, but the sand is too real, too warm. So I let go of the fight.

I smile, then laugh—a deep belly laugh that feels as foreign as it does necessary. I can't help it. Here I am, lying on a beach, blindfolded, with my stiff arm suddenly free. The absurdity of it fills me with joy. The man next to me is crying, which only makes me laugh harder. *Of course he's crying—we're here to heal. Isn't that the point?* But the fact that I'm not the one crying—that's what really gets me. Lately, it feels like I've been crying over everything.

Then I see them—my friends, dancing along the shoreline, their feet leaving prints in the sand as they spin and laugh. Their joy is magnetic, infectious. I realize they've been here all along, waiting for me to notice. And suddenly, it hits me: *How silly of me*. I can access this feeling anytime. The beach isn't a place—it's a state of mind. You don't have to be on a beach to feel like you're on one.

After this realization, I allow myself to sink into this healing sensation for as long as I need.

THEN, I'm off the beach and at the bottom of a staircase. As I begin to ascend, I feel a cloak settle onto my shoulders. With each step, I admire the colorful jewels adorning my fingers. *"I must be royalty,"* I think to myself, feeling like a character from *Bridgerton*, perhaps Queen Charlotte herself.

Once I reach the top and sit on my throne, I notice someone near the bottom of the steps. It's Tripp, but somehow, I don't recognize him. As I focus, I think, *"Oh, that happened? I must have had beer goggles on that night."* It's as if our time together was a fleeting moment, like a one-night stand. No attachment to him as a husband. I zoom out, and in the grand scheme of things, he feels like just a blip on the radar.

I see Lizzy, the paramour, standing beside him. A wave of love washes over me. *"Thank you, thank you for distracting him. I'm so grateful for you."*

I turn to Tripp and say, "Thank you for our son. I'm grateful for you. Now, I need you to go. I have so many things to do in this life." And just like that, they vanish, leaving me in a state of relaxed bliss.

I feel the need to relieve myself and, with some assistance, slowly walk to the bathroom. This is the same bathroom where I had once been so sick, endlessly googling about Emrata's separation. As I sit on the toilet, it takes a moment to begin, but once I do, I rejoice in the release. It's as though I'm not just emptying my bladder, but releasing everything stored in my body—my stomach, my mind. I am finally in my body.

Urinating feels almost orgasmic, and I thank my body as I release for what feels like hours. I never imagined feeling such pleasure from something so simple. When I steady myself at the sink, tears come, hard and unbidden.

"Thank you for conspiring for my benefit. Thank you, thank you, thank you!"

A swirl of memories floods my mind—the moment I met Elara, how we became roommates, the times we manifested our dreams together, the premonitions I had about this brownstone, Elara and James trying to help Tripp, us at court, the medicine urging James to connect with me, how he brought Evangeline into my life, all of it leading me here. I feel overwhelming love for James.

When I return to my mat, I lock eyes with James and mouth, with all my heart, "I LOVE YOU SO FUCKING MUCH!" He mouths the same back. It's a love so intense, born of the paths we've taken to heal, both separately and together.

The music gently pulls us back into our individual journeys. But I can still hear his giggles, and before I know it, I'm giggling too. We're both in the back of the room, while most others are crying, deep in their healing. James and I, though, are laughing like mischievous high schoolers. It feels silly, but also freeing.

I see scenes of myself laughing, almost as if I'm performing on *SNL* with Remy. It's a part of me I've forgotten, not by choice, but by necessity, a survival tactic to protect myself.

"I'm so sorry I forgot about you," I whisper to this forgotten part of me. "I won't forget you again."

I curl into myself, as if returning to the womb, and weep. It's a sorrow so deep it feels almost excruciating—like the pain of being separated from my son for centuries, and then suddenly being reunited.

In a flash, I am transported to my current living room, observing myself and my son as though I'm looking through a window. I watch myself, staring sadly into my phone while my son plays on the floor. He glances up at me from time to time, and I can hear his silent wish for me to join him. I know I should get down and play, but my body feels like a heavy weight of pain.

Then, he begins flapping his arms like a bird or a dragon, laughing, and saying, "Lift off, lift off!" At last, I put down my phone and join him, flapping my arms and making a "caw-caw" sound. He looks at me with a smile, his eyes sparkling, inviting me to continue. I get down on all fours, and he climbs onto my back. We become a dragon-bird hybrid, belly laughing over and over.

As I watch this scene, I notice a new vibration beginning to shift the energy in the room. I feel the ripple effect of this energy extending to my neighbors above me, then out into the sky. The playful energy I share with my son creates a high-frequency vibration that sinks deep into the Earth. I sense that Mother Earth can feel our frequencies, and it brings her comfort. It's like the warmth of the sun breaking through the clouds on a cold day—an easing of everything. I understand, in that moment, that how I act, think, and play can influence everything around me—from the sky above to the depths of the Earth, and back again.

Suddenly, Jude and I burst through the huge glass doors off the back deck of Elara and James's brownstone, riding on a massive swan. This swan represents Elara and James's unborn daughter. For some reason, I've always seen their daughter as a swan—spiritual, intuitive, beautiful, graceful, full of wisdom, and fearless. This vision, I realize, is to assure them that she will arrive safely and will be a force to be reckoned with.

From this glorious scene, I see myself holding my "scarcity mindset"—my fear of not having enough financially. I'm kneeling in my backyard, next to my flower garden, handing my fear over to Mother Earth.

"Thank you, my child," Mother Earth says. "It's now mine to handle." I watch the scarcity mindset being absorbed by the soil and transmuted by the Earth, almost like a filter system, changing metal into gold. It's being turned into something good. I place my hands in the soil, thanking her once more.

AS THE PSILOCYBIN begins to wear off, a deep hunger grabs my attention. I lost my appetite long ago due to stress, so this sensation is both new and distracting. When the ceremony ends, we are led into the main living room where Elara and James have prepared a spread of abundant snacks, from delicious fruits to chocolate. I'm in heaven. It feels like I'm eating for the first time. I can't believe how spectacular an apple tastes. My stomach moans in gratitude as it is finally being fed.

After filling my belly, we gather one last time for an integration circle. As the others mingle, a wave of overwhelming exhaustion begins to creep into my system. I grab my blanket and stumble up the spiral staircase to Elara's room, yearning for silence. Once I reach the bedroom, I lie down and pass out, not even getting a chance to say goodbye or thank Evangeline for everything. I don't wake again for almost nine hours.

12/4/23

MY PLAN B

"Love betters what is best" ~ *William Wordsworth*

The air is still, and the echo of footsteps clacks against my ears as the sound bounces off the cold concrete walls of the courthouse. My legs are crossed, my upper body stiff from tension, but I try my best to keep breathing, allowing my newly found belly to drop with each inhale. There's an urgency to relieve myself—oddly comforting—but I can't move until I see Celeste. I keep my eyes low, knowing that any moment now, I might make contact with my ex.

This is the last meeting before our divorce proceedings head to trial. We've been required to come in person, even though all of our previous court dates have been virtual. I'm sure the judge is trying to get us to settle, but I'm caught in a strange mixture of uncertainty and clarity about how we ended up here.

My ex refuses to sign the papers, yet he hasn't paid child support or initiated visitation in five months. I can't live like this anymore. I've secured my housing in Ohio, and I'm going. Celeste has contacted Tripp several times on this issue, but here we are, stuck.

A long hallway stretches before me, benches secured against the light wooden walls, nestled between courtrooms and conference rooms. Tripp has been representing himself, and I've heard through the grapevine that Merrick has been asking for more money for representation. Honestly, I don't care what the reason is for Merrick being off the case. I just hope I never have to see his despicable face again.

"DO you object to her request for relocation?" the judge asks.

"No, ma'am," Tripp replies.

"I hereby grant the motion for the plaintiff to relocate to Ohio," the judge continues, her voice filled with legal jargon that starts to blur in my ears. A high-pitched sound fills my right ear, sharp and dizzying, making me feel disconnected from everything around me. *"Am I really here?"* I wonder. *"Did he really just agree?"* I ask myself.

The gavel sounds, and the judge leaves the podium. As she descends, I begin to return to reality, my senses realigning.

"Did he agree for me to relocate? Did that just happen?" I ask Celeste quietly in her ear. She nods without breaking her gaze forward. Internally, I know I should feel victorious, but I don't. There's a sense of relief, but it's buried under disbelief. I never imagined he'd allow it without a fight.

Now, it's just the clerk, Tripp, myself, and Celeste. Celeste explains that the clerk will act as a mediator of sorts, to understand the remaining issues holding up the divorce. I nod, still in shock that I'm free to go, but also aware that there's more to settle.

"I want to start by saying that I never wanted this divorce. I don't want to divorce, and I don't believe she wants this divorce either," Tripp says.

I immediately make eye contact with the clerk and silently mouth, "Yes, I do." She doesn't react but maintains a composed expression, though I know she's processing everything, understanding the weight of what I've been through.

"*Thank you for our son. I'm so grateful for you. Now, I need you to go. I have many things to do in this life,*" I think to myself, repeating exactly what I said during the ceremony. I mean every word. I am grateful for Tripp, but it's time for this to end. I send him the message, "*It's time to be done,*" through the quiet transmission of my thoughts.

In a matter of minutes, the clerk confirms everything Celeste had already explained—everything I'm giving up to get him to sign. The final, biggest issue comes when he insists I pay him for half of his debt. The clerk asks if he can prove that this debt was used to support the family. Once that challenge is raised, Tripp backs down. We've agreed to all points. Now, we just need to finalize the terms and sign off.

"WHAT?? You're kidding me? The judge signed off on it? Hallelujah, praise the Lord!" my mom shrieks into the phone.

"Thank God, almighty," my dad's voice echoes from the background. It sounds like a celebration has erupted, and I hear my sister's voice, full of disbelief, coming through the line next.

"Justice has been served! See, Mere, good does prevail," my mom says, her voice full of encouragement. Her words are true, and part of me wants to believe in the justice, the closure, but it's hard to feel that way right now. I'm still numb, still processing.

"Mom, I know. I know this is true, but this is my life, and even though this is a positive outcome, it just feels so painful," I reply, aware of the undercurrent of disappointment in my voice. I know everyone wants me to be happier, but I'm not there yet. Not yet.

I know, deep down, that this is the best thing for me, for our son, and even for Tripp. I know Tripp understands he can't be what Jude needs right now, that Jude deserves to be in a place with more support, surrounded by his grandparents. I'm ultimately grateful for that, but I can't shake the devastation. I'm devastated that Tripp didn't fight harder, that he didn't choose to get sober. That keeping us in NYC, keeping this family together, wasn't as important as everything else he chose.

Once Jude falls asleep, I howl, my body wracked with hyperventilating sobs, like some animal in agony.

"I know this is for the best, I know, I know," I cry out to the Universe, "it just hurts so fucking badly." I try to reach for what I learned during the ceremony—the calm, the understanding that all is well—but the grip of pain tightens, and I can't seem to get there.

My stomach keeps contracting, knotting with every tear, but I try to encourage it to release, like I did before. Eventually, when the clenching becomes too much, I feel it give way, and I collapse, pressing my right cheek onto the cold bathroom tiles to ground myself long enough to catch my breath.

"*Our family is really over. I don't want this. I don't want this to be real. How, God? How the fuck could you let this happen? If you're even real, HOW??*"

Towels and robes hang on the bathroom door, and I kick at them, raging against the helplessness. I don't care about the neighbors upstairs; they can go fuck themselves. I will wail like an infant, scream like a teenager, for as long as I want.

I drag myself to my feet, planning to kick the door one more time, but I never make it. My head falls back against the tiles.

Eventually, I open my eyes, realizing I've exhausted myself to the point of possibly concussing myself. Another low, another reminder that I'm not Catwoman. I'm just a heartbroken wreck, desperate for release. *I give up.*

SUNSHINE POURS THROUGH THE WINDOW, casting a soft glow

on the room. My son climbs on top of me, his small weight and radiant smile a soothing balm for my soul.

"We're moving to Ohio, baby!" I say with a smile. "Where gamma and papa live!"

"Ohio, Ohio," he repeats, excited, darting toward the kitchen for breakfast before school.

I surprise myself with how much joy I feel, especially considering the state I was in just hours ago. My eyelids are swollen, my head is pounding, but in this moment, I feel something shifting inside me. I am ready to start fresh. To take control of my life.

I PARK my car on the bustling street, neatly aligned with my son's school. Through the rearview mirror, I catch glimpses of hurried lives passing by. When the flow of traffic slows, I jump out of the car.

As I circle around to the back, I notice a large piece of trash on the ground. I continue to open the door to unbuckle Jude. He steadies himself in the seat, and as he shifts to get out, I realize he might land right on the trash. I step to the side to kick it out of the way—then I freeze.

There, by my car's door, lies an unwelcome guest: an empty One Step Plan B box.

"*Are you fucking serious?*" I think, the vibrant purple, green, and white rainbow above the logo twisting in my gut, igniting a wave of nausea.

"Wait just a moment, my love," I whisper, my voice gentle, though the rage in my chest bubbles up. Without thinking, I kick the plastic box onto the sidewalk, quickly turning back to my son.

He propels himself into my arms, wrapping his little body around me with a hug.

We cross the street together, and he runs ahead, eager for school. "Have a good day!" I call after him, but as I turn away, my smile fades, replaced by a dark scowl.

"*Fuck that fucking Plan B box,*" I think to myself. I head straight for it but pause for a moment to glance over my shoulder, making sure none of the perfect parents can see me, hoping I'm positioned just right so the side of my car hides me slightly.

"Ok, Universe, what the fuck is this about?" I mutter under my breath as I unleash my rage on the box, each stomp a battle cry against the injustices of the world. I stomp the shit out of the plastic until the wet leaves that were once stuck to the bottom of my shoes are now intertwined with the increasingly soggy cardboard.

I take a breath, remembering box breathing. I count for four beats as I breathe in, then hold for four more. That's when I hear a car door slam nearby. It's fucking Sally. She's watching me, eyes wide, slowly putting on her seatbelt. I just glare back at her. "This bitch is always watching me, I swear," I mutter as I pick up the decapitated box and toss it onto the nearest lawn. Let someone else deal with this trash now.

Slipping into the driver's seat, the weight of the world settles on my shoulders, suffocating in its intensity. Outside, the world is blurred, reality slipping through my fingers, much like the day I woke up in my parents' yard.

"Please, please help me," I plead alone in my car, hoping something—anything—will make this okay. The tension in my throat starts to dissipate, and I think of the ceremony and the lessons I learned. I hear Evangeline's voice in my ear: "What is this experience signaling to you?"

It's confirmation to go. If a smashed-up box of Plan B right outside my son's door isn't a sign from the Universe to fucking go, I don't know what is!

I look around, smile, and laugh, saying, "Thank you for this confirmation! Thank you, Plan B! I'm getting the FUCK out of here."

A YEAR AGO, my credit score was close to 800, I had savings, and I had paid off all my debt. I was so proud of that accomplishment. Now, I'm here with a diminishing credit score, huge minimum payments, and a shrinking credit limit—all for the sake of my freedom. My freedom is worth that, and deep in my bones, I know I can bet on myself to turn it all around. I am that arrow, and life is pulling me back really, really far. I imagine that right when I'm stretched too thin, life will launch me forward, further than I can ever imagine. I can't look to the right or left because I'm not living anyone else's life. I have friends taking vacations, buying second homes, and starting renovations, and it's none of my concern. Mother Earth taught me to hand over my fears, and she will alchemize it all for me.

While I know I will be taken care of financially, I also need to be realistic about my limits. Right now, I don't have enough to fly back and look at apartments in person, so I choose the best one for Jude and me from FaceTime open houses.

My biggest priority is making sure Jude feels comfortable when he arrives at the new apartment. I plan for my parents to drive all his most important items from NY to Ohio before our arrival. I want the big items, like beds and tables, to be set up by someone else since my parents have already done so much. I hire someone from TaskRabbit to assemble the beds, and I get them delivered from a budget furniture store, along with side tables from Amazon. This way, when my parents arrive with Jude's things, the rooms are ready to be decorated.

When my son was tiny, I came across an amazing large print of a blue parrot on sale. Jude had been obsessed with *Little Einsteins*, and this particular tropical bird from one of the shows was his favorite. I want that picture to be the centerpiece of his bedroom, with all the other decorations made to fit around it. I know my mom will be able to find perfect items from the thrift store, adding personal and unique touches to his new room.

When we finally arrive at our new home, the carpeted steps leading to the second floor immediately captivate Jude. While the carpet wasn't my first choice aesthetically, his delight and safety make it worthwhile. As he eagerly reaches the top, I ask, "Are you ready to see your new room?!" Without a word, he walks down the hallway and finds it, directly across from mine.

He spots the tropical bird picture, initially confused, but then his face lights up with excitement as he realizes it's his bird picture from home! He climbs onto the bed and starts jumping. I exhale.

"Look! You even have your own door that you can shut!" I exclaim. In our New York apartment, what was advertised as a two-bedroom was actually a one-bedroom with an additional space right off our room, probably intended as a sitting area or office. Jude didn't have true privacy since he had no door. This had always troubled me because, as he grew older, I knew he would need his own space. When money spent on substances began affecting our finances and straining our marriage, I knew the dream of giving Jude a real bedroom seemed more and more out of reach, causing me immense anxiety about the future. I always believed I could give my son a better childhood than my own, and as the years went by, not being able to provide this one essential thing weighed heavily on me. Yet, here we are now.

Fast forward to evening, and I lie in bed. I feel an overwhelming sense of peace wash over me. Our new home is quiet, and the only sounds are the faint hum of the little neighborhood outside and the gentle rustle of wind. My room, now fully furnished and cozy, mirrors Jude's room just down the hall. We have arranged our beds in the same way, angled so that we can see each other through the open doors.

From my bed, I can see Jude tucked in under his favorite blanket, the soft glow of his nightlight casting comforting shadows on the walls. His eyes flutter closed, and a sense of contentment fills the air. Knowing he feels safe and secure in his new room brings me immense joy.

As I watch him, my heart swells with relief and gratitude. The anxiety and stress of the past months melts away. I watch Jude's breathing slow as he drifts into sleep, his small chest rising and falling rhythmically.

I let my own eyes close, feeling the cool sheets against my skin and the softness of my pillow cradling my head. It is a simple, yet powerful moment—being able to watch my son fall asleep down the hall, knowing we are both safe and comfortable in our new space. The connection between us feels stronger than ever, even though we aren't sharing the same bed.

As I drift off to sleep, I know that whatever the future holds, we have found a new sense of home, together.

Part VII

"He who hasn't tasted bitter things hasn't earned sweet things" ~ *Gottfried Wilhelm Leibniz*

12/23/23

REVIVAL

"To begin, begin" ~ William Wordsworth

I've officially settled in Ohio, and this Christmas, I only have a short two-hour drive south to celebrate with my parents. Reflecting on how much my life has changed since last Christmas, I find gratitude in my growth. I've come to appreciate myself more—for how I parent, advocate, and love. In that vein, I've made a conscious decision to be kinder and gentler with myself, starting with stopping birth control.

To clarify, I had my fallopian tubes removed to prevent pregnancy due to health risks. Yet, I found myself back on birth control after the fact. I realize now that I had been convinced that I was to blame for my family's troubles. I was told I was uptight and too demanding since the surgery. I blamed my depression, deep loneliness, and crying spells on my hormones and didn't want to face the truth; that I was being severely emotionally and physically neglected. Thing is, I was blamed for the same things whether I was on birth control or not.

I have come to the sobering fact that I was gaslit (both by my husband and myself). By letting go of the pill and the "emotional and demanding" narrative I had co-signed with my ex, I can let new feelings and sensations into my body without harsh judgment. Although my period has been initially unpredictable, I truly feel that I can feel again, especially sexual feelings that have been dormant for so long.

And I mean, we are talking, all the time. And inappropriately so! Even now, I'm scrolling on Instagram and the latest Calvin Klein ad featuring Jeremy Allen White suddenly makes me feel a bit tingly around my lady parts. I am initially not happy about this since he allegedly cheated on his ex-wife right after she had their two kids, which obviously resonates with me. So when I get turned on by said alleged cheater running across the rooftops of NYC while stripping down to his tidy whities, I can't help but conclude that I am exceptionally sexually frustrated (and confused).

Then, I realize the song to which he is running across those rooftops is "You Don't Own Me." Hearing the tune, I immediately sit up. As a child, I had two favorite movies—*Billy Madison* and *The First Wives Club*. Why I gravitated toward these movies, I'm not sure, but I had recently been discussing the similarities between my current life and *The First Wives Club*.

"There's no way this commercial is set to 'You Don't Own Me,'" I say to myself while watching, and I smirk. Siri must have been listening in while I was talking about *The First Wives Club*.

I type into Google—Jeremy Allen White Calvin Klein song—and sure enough, the commercial was actually filmed to it.

I get sucked back into his abs, his eyes, and those tight boxers, and then notice I'm excited again. I decide to take care of this because I don't want to be rewatching this video all day.

Once I feel my body release, I feel clear headed again and well, my whole body feels really divine. Better than it has in a super long time. Is this the pleasure I have been missing? I realize that the truth is, these hormones are allowing me to feel again and that means I'm coming alive again. It's like the scene in the last season of *Sex & the*

City when Samantha encourages Smith to have sex while on location since she has lost her libido from cancer treatment. Smith explains that her libido is like the seasons; she's in winter and just because the leaves are gone does not mean the trees are dead. He later gifts her some budding flowers with a note that says, "Looking forward to spring."

This is how I feel. My libido has been in hiding, not ready to come out until it felt safe to emerge. I have not lost it. It is all coming back. With that in mind, I decide to let myself experience even more pleasure. And that means experiencing pleasure with the potential involvement of someone else.

I DECIDE to scroll through Hinge—that's a dating app for anyone that isn't familiar. I am feeling good about myself. I am ready to be touched.

When I try to envision what a future partner would even be like, I get a flash of a dark haired man with stubble, and a baseball cap backward, with glasses, leaning in for a kiss as I return to my work on the computer. While I can't make out the exact facial features, the feeling coming from this man is, "I adore you." He doesn't adore just my body, my lips, my career, my money (or lack thereof), no—he adores my true self.

This "vision" flashes in front of me every couple months when I allow myself to daydream about a potential love life. In truth, I feel freaked out by the thought of a man coming into my life because I don't want to mess up the groove I have found with Jude. "I love my life," I often say. "They'd have to be amazing for me to let anyone in."

I scroll through the app and begin to X almost everyone. No one is doing it for me. Then, there is a man that catches my eye with his chocolate eyes. They look delicious. Huge smile that I want to see in real life. Dark hair, peppered with white that creates perfect curls on his head. Yum.

Ok, the first picture grabs my attention, now—let the digging for the red flags commence!

"44"...That's okay, good for him to be older.

"Previously lived in NYC"....Hmm glad he's lived outside of Ohio.

"From Wisconsin"...probably boring.

"Drinks sometimes, but doesn't smoke weed"...yea, he's probably boring.

"Has children"...looks like a good dad but anyone can on a dating app. I bet he spends zero time with them.

"Not afraid of distance"...def red flag. All I hear is, "I got hoes in different area codes."

"Has been on a CBS reality tv show, but you likely haven't' watched it"...hmm, it's probably *Survivor*. The only time I've purposely gone onto *CBS.com* is to watch *Survivor*. My mom has loved *Survivor* since season 1, and I grew up watching it with her. Even when I moved out of my parents house, we'd separately watch *Survivor* then call each other after to discuss. That show kept us connected.

"Picture of him with a unicorn horn on his head, along with his daughter"...cuteeeee but again, it's probably the one time he saw her that month.

Then I scroll to the last pic.

"Picture with his daughters, flannel on, hat on backwards"... damn. He's a hot dad.

I send him a like and thankfully, he had already liked me, so we instantly match! Yes!!

A FEW DAYS pass and I check if this man named Matteo has responded. Nope. He has not. I will wait and stalk.

Friday, Dec. 29th

ME: *"Thanks for the like! I feel like we would definitely get along 😊 Btw, was it survivor?"*

"Also, I can't stop looking at your profile. Eyes, smile, voice, I like it all."

Wow, I was bold. He doesn't respond so, of course, I shoot my shot again.

Tuesday, Jan. 2nd

ME: *"Hi, I am going to take a break from Hinge so if you ever see this and feel inclined to contact me, my number is _____"*

Thursday, Jan. 4th

Still no word. Well, he is clearly playing hard to get. I feel like a sexual lioness, one that will be given the attention she deserves and I am not ashamed to hunt him down for it. I will give him two more days to text me, then I will stalk him again.

Saturday, Jan. 6th

ME: *"I can not believe I keep coming back on here every couple of days to see if you've seen this. I feel crazy! I just moved back to Columbus from NYC and the hinge options are scary, haha. Your eyes are just so kind."*

That is the truth. I know it deeply that he is kind and for the first time...maybe...ever...I consciously am going toward the good.

Finally, he replies. He explains that he rarely checks the apps and that my messages are a pleasant surprise, instead of acknowledging how they are also borderline stalkerish. We settle on a meeting place and I nervously wait for my first date in Ohio.

"I WAS on Youtube for something and saw you were going live so I caught the tail end of it. You're so great, and pretty, and great, and pretty," Matteo texts to me.

He is so good with his words. I have a hard time taking this compliment. This sort of support has been absent in my life for many years before the actual divorce. There are two feelings existing at once. On one hand, I feel emotional and grateful that I've met him; I know he's been divinely guided into my life and that I absolutely deserve him. On the other hand, I feel irritable and frustrated. I have no idea why. I sit on the couch for a moment and instead of pushing this feeling away, I let the irritability wash over me. I tell it—yes, out loud—that it's welcome here.

"You have a right to feel irritated," I tell myself. Just then, a pang of sadness pours over me as tears begin to stream. I feel sorrow for my old self that settled for so little. His words go so far, why did I ever accept so much less? Why did I ever beg for appreciation and acknowledgement from someone that was absolutely unworthy of my love?

A few minutes pass and I move into angered love; that's the only way to describe it. I am angry in defense of the love I now have for myself. A love I'd want my friends and loved ones and really anyone to feel so they protect themselves. I'm only going to lean into the people that see this in me.

1/14/24

IT'S JUST MONEY

"No man is an island, entire of itself; every man is a piece of the continent, a part of the main." ~ John Donne

"They want another $3,000?" my mom shrieks, her voice slicing through the quiet like a knife. It's not a question, really; it's an announcement of outrage. The final-finalizing of my divorce comes with yet another bill, and my retainer is dry. I feel my chest tighten. I've got nothing left—no savings, no credit, no lifeline.

The shame crashes in before I can stop it. My face crumples as the tears spill over, unstoppable. I can't hold it together like I usually do in front of my parents. I've spent my whole life as the strong one, the child who has her act together, who doesn't need help. But here I am, crumbling, exposed, and it feels like I'm letting them down in real time.

"I was supposed to be more than this," I sob, the words ripping out of me. "I feel like such a loser. How did my life end up like this? I don't know how to swing it."

From the other room, my dad stands silently, listening. His presence looms like a storm cloud, unpredictable. I brace myself for the flash of frustration I've come to expect, the kind that reminds me I'm asking too much. But instead, his voice cuts through the air, steady and calm.

"We'll cover the $3,000," he says.

I lift my head, certain I've misheard him. "What?"

He steps closer, still calm. "Don't worry about the money. We just need to get you divorced so you can move on and get back on track."

It's such a matter-of-fact statement, so plain and kind, that it takes me a second to process it. A lump rises in my throat, but it's not from sadness this time. It's something softer, warmer. I shake my head, unsure how to respond.

"Dad, I can't," I stammer. "I'm 39 years old. I'm not a kid. I don't want to take money from you."

"Mere, it's just money," he says, his tone surprisingly gentle. He shrugs, almost playful, "What else are we going to spend it on?" His words carry the lightness of a joke, but they land like a balm. For the first time in months, I feel the weight on my chest begin to shift.

"Really? Are you sure?" I ask, tears still spilling but with a new flavor—relief. "I'll pay you back. It might take a while, but I'll do it."

"Don't worry about it," he says, brushing off the idea like it's inconsequential. "Now, no more fussing over this idiot. Let's just get this done."

His words don't feel dismissive—they feel solid, grounding, like he's giving me permission to lean on him. And weirdly, that makes me feel stronger. He knows what it's like to stare down a dollar amount and feel like it's an impossible cliff to scale. And maybe, just maybe, he knows how much it means for someone to step in and say, *I'll carry this one for you.*

There's a quiet moment between us where I feel something inside me shift, something small but significant. A little piece of me, long-hidden and frayed, begins to stitch itself back together.

2/14/24

EROS & ATHENA

"I to myself am dearer than a friend" ~ Shakespeare

It's February 14th, 2024—Valentine's Day. Today, I'll appear in court to finalize my divorce.

It seems fitting that the divorce wraps up on this day. While Valentine's is linked to Cupid, hearts, and love, its origins are far darker. Much like a crumbling marriage, the exact beginnings are murky, but all theories point to Rome.

One theory tells of a Roman priest named Valentine, who defied Emperor Claudius II's decree outlawing marriage for young men, believing they made better soldiers. Valentine continued to perform secret marriages and was eventually executed for his defiance.

Another theory suggests that Saint Valentine of Terni, a bishop, was the true namesake. He too was beheaded by Claudius II and allegedly sent a letter signed, "From your Valentine" before his death —a phrase still used today. Despite the uncertainty of these legends, they paint Valentine as a sympathetic and romantic figure.

If there's anything I've learned, it's that fighting for love is often futile and can lead to various forms of death: the death of naivety, trust, family, and ultimately, love itself.

Somehow, Greek mythology merged with Valentine's Day, bringing Cupid into the mix. Cupid, or Eros, is depicted as a mischievous cherub who, with his golden arrows, can make people fall in love or fall out of it just as easily. I wonder if my own marriage unraveled simply for the amusement of a capricious child.

THE VIRTUAL MEETING was set for 2:30 pm. It's now 2:42 pm, and there's no sign of Tripp.

"What if he doesn't show?" I text Celeste, slipping my phone under the computer.

"Ugh. They'll probably ask us to come back," she replies.

"Ugh," I text back, feeling my whole body tense.

"Of course he is pulling this, he hasn't taken the process seriously," Celeste responds.

"Can I at least say that I wasn't under duress?" I text Celeste, hoping that she can encourage the judge to let me vouch for my part without Tripp being present.

"I can ask," she responds.

"Please. I don't want to come back," I text frantically. The whole court process has been nothing short of traumatizing. Every moment churns my stomach and I anticipate another postponement, another fight.

The judge agrees and asks me to raise my right hand. It takes me a moment to remember my right from left.

"Do you swear that the evidence you are about to give will be the truth, the whole truth, and nothing but the truth, so help you God?"

"I do."

The next questions go quickly.

"Please state your full name for the court"

"What's your spouse's name?"

"How long have you been married?"

"Were you or your spouse a resident in New York six months before the filing?"

"Yes."

"Why are you seeking a divorce?"

"Irreconcilable differences."

"Do you have any children born or adopted during the marriage?

"Yes."

"What are the names and dates of birth of the minor children?"

I answer shakily.

"Do you sign this agreement freely and voluntarily without any duress?"

I hesitate because I've been under duress the whole time.

"Yes."

"Do you still desire a final judgment for the dissolution of the marriage?"

"Yes.

"Does this agreement resolve any and all marital assets and liabilities and the minor children?"

"Yes."

"Is there anything left for the court to decide?"

"I don't believe so."

"Are you asking the court to order that you and your spouse abide by this agreement?"

"Yes."

"Are you asking the court to enter a final judgment dissolving your marriage?"

"Yes."

Just as I finish, the clerk notifies the judge that Tripp has arrived, twenty minutes late. He is unable to connect with video, still, the judge approves him to speak via phone.

On the one hand, I'm relieved to not see his face. On the other, I find this odd; doesn't she need to see that he's actually raising his right hand? Ultimately, this is the perfect ending because it is indicative of how this entire process has gone. He hasn't had to really show his face, he has gotten to dodge drug tests and deflect responsibility. He gets to do as little as possible, disrespecting not only me, but the court, and still, nobody says anything about it. I can feel my anger but I just want this over with.

I hold my breath while he answers the same questions asked of me. The hearing concludes abruptly and everyone leaves the online session.

I sit still, unsure of what to do.

"Soooo, that's it?" I ask myself out loud, confused by the hurried simplicity of it all.

A few moments pass then I ring Celeste.

"So, what's next?" I ask Celeste.

"Nothing, there's nothing else for you to do. I'll draft up the final agreement that will need to be submitted in the next two weeks or so and the judge will sign off on it," Celeste explains.

"Wait, is there a chance he won't sign again?" I ask, never believing fully it could be finally done.

"It's doubtful after this final hearing since he gave testimony. I anticipate that it'll take several months for the final divorce decree to be signed," she explains.

"Several months? Ugh, I want this over,"

"It's just waiting, the hardest part is over. No more court appearances, it's done," she says.

"Thank you, Celeste."

I decide to stop by Whole Foods to gather some groceries before picking up my son from school. There are heart cookies on display and flowers for sale. I get some red velvet cupcakes to enjoy with Jude later, along with some flowers.

We get home after devouring the cupcakes in the car and I sit down to write myself a Valentine's Day card. Instead of this being in the name of St. Valentine, I will be denouncing my love today, all in the name of Freedom.

Dear Meredith,

May you experience the birth of freedom, confidence, power, fire, hope, and especially, peace.

Your Valentine,

Meredith

"OH SHIIIIIT," I mutter to myself as I struggle to button my favorite jean shorts. My thighs are bulging out the sides, and I've got a sizable camel toe. "Eww," I say aloud. The situation feels almost comical as I waddle to the mirror for a better look. I've definitely gotten the ass I always wanted, but it came with a pooch and a pair of booming thunder thighs. I feel almost cartoonish, my curves so exaggerated.

"Some people would die to have your body," my friend reminds me. I look back skeptically at her and return to the mirror. "Your body is recalibrating. Can you give yourself space to just be how you are?"

The divorce had worn me away, stress gnawing at me until my once healthy frame had turned gaunt and fragile. Back then, each jutting bone was a testament to sleepless nights and tear-soaked pillows, the physical manifestation of a life unraveling.

But now, almost two years later, I am different. I have found a new home, a sanctuary that cradles me with warmth and safety. Here, I have begun to heal and rebuild. The weight I had lost in despair has returned, slowly at first, then with a boom!

I trace a finger along the curve of my hip, my mind whispering cruel remnants of past insecurities. I remember the sharpness of my collarbones, how they had once seemed to cut through the air like the words of my ex-husband. Thinness had been a shield, a way to control something, anything, in a life that had spun out of control.

At first, I welcomed the weight gain. It was a sign that I was safe that I could breathe again. I no longer woke up with tightness in my chest, dreading the day ahead. Instead, I woke up to the sound of birds, the sun casting a golden glow through my bedroom window—a new beginning.

But embracing this new body is harder than I had expected. I turn sideways, observing the curve of my belly, the puffiness, the squishy feel of it. These changes, though symbols of my hard-won peace, still feel foreign, as if I inhabit someone else's skin.

"I know this weight means I'm healthy, that I'm healing, but it's hard to accept sometimes."

My friend reaches out, squeezing my hand gently. "Your body is a reflection of your journey. You're not just surviving anymore. You're living. These curves are the story of your strength and resilience. They're beautiful."

Later in the night, I stand before my mirror again, fully naked. My once flattened breasts have become full again, and I kind of like the shape my body makes without the confines of clothing. My pale skin seems to glow in the darkness, reminiscent of those honored in Renaissance art. I think back to when I studied in Florence, Italy, and saw *The Birth of Venus* for the first time. I remember thinking, *"I look like her when I'm naked."* In the time she lived, most people lived in poverty. Having extra weight and curves was a status symbol; it meant you had wealth and could eat to your satisfaction.

Then, I remember *Pallas and the Centaur*. A distinct smirk crosses my face as I recall it: Pallas is Athena. She is seen covered in olive branches, but it's a disguise, she is actually a warrior maiden. She grips the hair of the drunken centaur, Nessus, who tried to kidnap her, underestimating her power. She looks down on him in his pathetic, drunken state. Athena doesn't kill Nessus; he meets his fate later when Hercules shoots him with a poisoned arrow after attempting to assault his new bride, Deianira. He should've known better.

Remembering Athena and her power gives me peace about my body. As I put on an oversized t-shirt and underwear before heading to bed, I think how Athena's curves were probably the least of her worries. Since I too have survived a drunken man, maybe they should also be the least of mine.

IT'S two days after Valentine's Day, and Matteo is making the hour-and-a-half trek to see me while Jude is at school. Honestly, the fact that he's willing to drive all that way just for lunch feels like some kind of miracle. In a world where men are mostly texting "u up?" at 2 am, this is practically a grand gesture.

We had one great first date back in early January, but life, as it does, got in the way. Between his kids, my kid, and both of us juggling busy schedules, finding time to meet up again felt like trying to assemble IKEA furniture without the instructions. We texted here and there, but it wasn't until now that the stars—and our calendars—finally aligned. And yet, even with the time and distance, he's stayed consistent with quiet patience and steady effort.

When I open the door, there he is, standing like some kind of rom-com hero—tall, slightly windblown, and holding the biggest bouquet of wildflowers I've ever seen. Not roses—wildflowers. The kind that look like they were plucked from a sun-drenched meadow, just like the ones on my wallpaper. And here's the thing: it's not just that he brought flowers, it's that he *noticed* the wallpaper... from watching my YouTube videos. He notices things. I'm not sure whether to swoon or laugh at the absurdity of it all—probably both.

"I know you've had a really hard week, and I wanted to do something special," he says, handing me the bouquet with a sheepish grin that makes my heart do this weird, flutter thing. It's almost enough to make me forget that two days ago I was signing divorce papers and trying not to spiral into a pit of existential dread.

Almost.

I set the flowers down—carefully, because I'm going to want to stare at them later and remind myself that men like Matteo actually exist—and step closer to him. My arms find their way around his neck, and when he pulls me in, it's like my whole body exhales. For the first time in days, I feel something other than tense. I feel...light. This is a surprising sensation since acquiring these new Athena curves...and I can tell he likes them.

As he grips my hips, a thought pops into my head, uninvited but welcome: *I feel safe with him.* It's a revelation, really—like realizing that maybe, just maybe, it's okay to trust this man who shows up, who notices, who drives one and a half hours just to take me to lunch and make me laugh. That's something worth holding on to.

4/2/24

CAPTAIN

"Fear not for the future, weep not for the past" ~ Percy Bysshe Shelley

One day, when Jude was 7 weeks old, I noticed that his morning nap was lasting longer than usual.

"That's weird," I muttered under my breath, watching his pouty lips and long lashes as he dozed.

"What's weird?" Tripp asked.

"He's just been sleeping longer than usual," I replied, my concern evident.

"Isn't this a good thing? It's great that he's sleeping more," he responded, a slight tinge of annoyance in his voice that only a wife can detect.

"I don't know. He should be waking out of hunger," I said.

"I'm sure it's fine," he reassured me..

"Something is off. His breathing seems slowed down," I said, hoping to trigger some concern in Tripp. "I'm gonna give him 30 more minutes max then, I don't know, we may need to take him to the doctor," I said, taking Jude's temperature again. Tripp continued to stare into his computer, not acknowledging my warning. He has always hated doctors and hospitals. He'll do anything to avoid them. It was a battle to get him to take the flu vaccine before Jude was born. He hasn't seen a doctor since he was 18. He passes out from blood draws, terrified of needles.

After fifteen minutes of watching every inhale and exhale from my little baby's chest, I decided to walk outside to get some air. I hobbled to the back deck, feeling the postpartum weight with every step. I stared up at the sky as my anxiety climbed.

"What should I do?" I asked myself, gazing at the cotton candy clouds above me.

Suddenly, I winced. A foreign feeling suddenly took over my body; a deep *deep* knowing that my child was not okay. It felt as if it was coming from the depths of the Earth, shaking my core foundation so that I would not turn away from it. It was demanding my attention and I had to honor it.

I burst back into the house, grabbing my purse, keys, and phone before heading to Jude. I began to pick his little body up when Tripp intervened.

"What are you doing? He's fine. Put him down, he probably just needs the sleep," he said to me, trying to diffuse my hurriedness.

"We are going to the ER. There's something wrong. You can either come with me or you can stay here," I told him. He knew I was serious.

Frustrated, he got dressed and headed with me to the car. He was irritated and backed out the driveway, hitting the side of the pavement, causing a jolt which made Jude and I bounce a little. Tripp is usually a good driver but I could feel that he was angry that we were headed to the ER right then. I wanted to yell at him, but I bit my tongue knowing it's not worth it. The only thing that mattered right then was getting to the hospital.

"Are you going to do this about every little thing? You know, you can't freak out over every single ailment," he said, condescendingly.

"I'm not freaking out over a little thing. I know there is something wrong, I can feel it," I replied. He audibly snorted, mocking me.

"Ok, you can "feel" it?" he scoffed.

"Look, if we get there and there's nothing wrong with him, which I hope is the case, then you can be mad at me all you want. It will be deserved and I'll happily defer to you in the future. But until we know for sure, you have to trust me, ok?" I said firmly.

"Ok," he replied, backing off. He reached his hand back to me and we interlocked our fingers. He squeezed my hand and said, "Love you."

"Love you," I responded, feeling his support.

"WE WILL BE ADMITTING your son due to a urinary tract infection. We will be administering intravenous antibiotics and will need to monitor him overnight," the ER doctor informed us.

Tripp and I just stared at the doctors, stunned by the diagnosis.

"It's a good thing you brought him in when you did. Urinary tract infections that occur under 3 months of age have a high risk of permanent kidney damage and sepsis."

"But he was only sleeping more than usual, he didn't display any other symptoms really," I responded in disbelief.

"It is surprising that he didn't have more symptoms because there is already swelling in his kidneys. It's hard with babies because they can't tell us how they feel and many symptoms go under the radar. That's why I always tell new parents that, when in doubt, go to the doctor. This is a perfect example of why it's important," the doctor explains.

Tripp looked at me with tears in his eyes and without any words; I could tell he was grateful for my persistence. We gripped each other's hands tightly as we watched the nurses begin to prepare him to be transferred.

Jude's urinary issues did not end there. He was referred to an urologist who found a blockage in his urethra and at 14 weeks old, so he underwent urethra surgery. After the surgery, he was in the hospital overnight. The doctor stated that there was debris in his bladder that was cleared as well at the bottleneck in his urethra. The urologist noted that if we will not consider circumcision, we should begin putting steroid cream on his foreskin three times a day to loosen it since it appeared to be tighter than most.

"Absolutely not," Tripp said.

"But Tripp, if we don't do it, there's a higher chance that he'll develop another UTI," I responded.

"No, it's child abuse. It originates from ritual mutilation. He can't consent to it and they can't prove that it's the reason he had a UTI," he stated.

"I don't disagree with you on the fundamental basis, but the doctor recommended it. Shouldn't we do anything to prevent issues for him down the road? He can't consent, but we are then the ones that must decide what is best for him" I pleaded.

"No, I won't agree to it. I'll make sure that he understands how to clean it and prevent any issues," he stated.

Inside, I wanted to push back again but I trusted my husband and this was one area he's passionate about, so I backed down.

IT IS April 2024 and signs of spring are finally appearing. I can feel it's a time of new beginnings. Yet, old issues are rearing their ugly heads (no pun intended).

"So, what brings you in?" the urologist asks.

"We just moved to Ohio from NY in December and I wanted to make sure Jude has a new urologist in the area, especially because he has been asking to go to the bathroom every thirty minutes at school and we think he may be in pain. He's been pulling on himself. I know kids do this at his age, but it's all the time. There's also an odor to his urine, I just want to make sure he's okay. I'm sure I'm being overly cautious but better safe than sorry, right?," I joke anxiously, fearing that I'm as crazy as Tripp had made me feel. "He's also autistic and delayed in speech, so it's hard to know what he's feeling. I try so many different things."

"I see in his chart that he had urinary surgery at 14 weeks old after a UTI?" the urologist asks.

"Yes. I try my best to get him to clean himself, but I can't guarantee it's up to par. He won't let me clean him, maybe because it hurts? Regardless, I don't want to cause him to have trauma around his penis," I say, half sarcastically, half truthfully.

"Let me do an exam to see what is going on."

After a quick examination, the doctor turns to me.

"My recommendation is that he gets circumcised, the sooner the better," the urologist says.

"Ok," I reply before exhaling.

"He has a serious case of phimosis. He just happens to be one of those few uncircumcised kiddos with an abnormally tight foreskin, which explains the odor. The urine is not being fully expelled, meaning some urine is sitting in the foreskin between bathroom breaks, leading to infection," the urologist states. "It sounds like he's been dealing with balanitis as well. That's when the foreskin is inflamed."

I can feel the tears welling up in my eyes. My poor boy! I hate that he's been having to deal with this.

"God, I feel horrible. I thought there was something wrong, but with his speech delay, it's so hard to get him to tell me how he's feeling," I say, beginning to let the tears pour.

"I have two boys and one is autistic too. Don't be hard on yourself. You are here now," she says. Her personal share means everything and I begin to calm myself.

She explains that recovery from the surgery is quick and she will make sure that he will be in the least amount of pain. She reassures me that he'll be in much less pain now than if I wait until he is older.

"Ok, how do I go about scheduling?"

"We will call you by the end of the week with times. It should be in the next couple of weeks," she states.

"I, thankfully, have full medical decision making, but," I pause, hesitating to bring it up, "I know that his father isn't going to be happy about it. We just finalized the divorce. He is very against circumcision," I say, starting to feel anxious.

"Whatever beliefs he has connected to circumcision do not matter, this is what is best for your son's health," she states while turning toward her computer. She is so matter-of-fact that I smile a little, surprised by her bluntness.

A feeling of pride and power rises in me as we leave the doctor's office.

I knew all along he needed this. *I* fought to protect him. All of the money spent, the time negotiating, in this moment, it is crystal clear —it was all worth it. I can finally reap what I sowed. It is finally tangible. I can swiftly make these imperative decisions without a fight, without a doubt, without abuse.

I'm the captain now.

4/19/24

3 QUESTIONS

"Soul meets soul on lovers lips." ~ Percy Blysshe Shelley

April 19th, 2024. The day Taylor Swift drops *The Tortured Poets Department,* a double album, sending the world into a frenzy. I am on my way to Cincinnati to see Matteo, who has agreed —somewhat enthusiastically—to watch the premiere of the "Fortnight" music video with me.

As I drive, a wave of exhaustion washes over me, not the kind that sleep can cure, but the kind that sinks into your bones. My eyes feel like they're carrying the weight of every sleepless night I've ever had. There's a throbbing at my temples, a subtle but persistent reminder that my body knows more than I do.

"Must be the sunshine," I tell myself as I slide on my sunglasses, though deep down, I know it's more than that. I pull off the highway, searching for something—anything—to snap me out of this fog. The resulting gas station is grimy, the air thick with the smell of body odor and old coffee. I scan the coolers: Starbucks Frappuccino, Monster, Celsius. None of them offer the solution I'm looking for, but I grab a Celsius anyway, hoping it will do the trick.

But as I near Cincinnati, I realize the caffeine hasn't touched the heaviness inside me. It's still there, clinging to me like an unwelcome guest. When I arrive, Matteo is already outside, waiting for me. He pulls me into a hug, his arms wrapping around me with a firmness that feels like both an invitation and a challenge.

I let myself sink into him, the way you sink into a warm bath after a long day. The scent of his cologne hits me, familiar and grounding, a reminder that there's still something solid in this spinning world. I breathe him in deeply, letting his presence anchor me.

His home is exactly as I remember it—full of Shepard Fairey prints, pieces of art, and pictures of his kids. I pull out the piece of paper for the "3 question game," something I discovered recently and have been itching to try with him. Matteo's eyes flicker with a mix of curiosity and concern.

I explain the game, how it's rooted in relational psychology, something I picked up from a Teal Swan video. I watch him process this, taking in my words while knowing this isn't just about the game. It's about what we're really doing here—two people trying to navigate the murky waters of connection, trust, and vulnerability.

"According to research, no matter what culture you are from or race you are born into, we all associate specific things with other 'things.' Basically, the associations can tell us a lot about each other," I say, noticing his hesitation. "Don't worry! I'll share my answers after," I say with a smile, realizing how much I enjoy making men nervous.

"But what if I chose the wrong answer?" Matteo asks.

"There are no wrong answers. This is for the purpose of understanding each other, but we will do it in an abstract way, almost taking it from our subconscious, ya know?"

"I'll take your word for it," he says with a laugh. He gets me a clean piece of paper and pen so that I can write down his answers and explanations.

"Let's begin," I say with a wink. "Matteo, what is your favorite color and three deep reasons why?"

"Oh man..." he says and looks up. He is staring at the ceiling for quite some time, not saying a word. "What is considered deep?" he asks.

"Like, nothing surface level. You want to go deep, really examine why you love the color," I explain. He closes his eyes again.

"But I change my favorite color all the time," he says, unsure of what to say.

"I will take note of that," I say jokingly. "Don't think too hard, just tell me what comes to mind for you."

When Teal discusses this exercise on YouTube, she says to take notice of everything. "If someone struggles to come up with a favorite color, they may struggle with knowing who they are or they may hate the feeling of being 'tied down' to being one way or another," I hear her voice say in my mind as I remember her teachings.

"Yellow," he says, "I would say yellow." I'm surprised and I'm not sure why.

"The first reason, umm, would be that it reminds me of the sun. When I was sitting in the airport this past week, I found a chair where the light was streaming in. It was shining on me. I sat back and closed my eyes, feeling the warmth. It was so refreshing, calming, energizing to me" he explains as I listen intently while writing his answers down. I could listen to him talk for hours, it's so soothing.

"The other reason is that the sun allows there to be light on the Earth and light equals life, it allows for life to grow and flourish. The third reason is because the yellow of the sun reminds me of happy memories, and those have usually been on the beach or near water, it's a gathering place for friends. So the yellow reminds me of being around loved ones and water."

"Beautiful," I say, "Ok, the next one is what is your favorite animal and three deep reasons why?"

Matteo takes time to really think.

"This is so hard, I love animals," he says. "But my first instinct, I think is an average answer, but it would be a dog."

"That's not average! If you love dogs, you love dogs!" I say. "Alright, give me the three reasons."

"Ok, the first reason would be companionship. Dogs are just so happy to see you when you come home and give raw, genuine love. The second reason is that I really enjoy taking care of them. I love being able to feed them, pet them, walk them, I just love caring for them," he says as my heart begins to turn to mush. "The third reason, is that some dogs, or really most dogs, have a smile. I love the smile that comes on dogs faces. Other animals have it too but I especially like the smile on dogs."

"Amazing answers," I say with a smile on my face. "See! This isn't too bad right?"

"No, it's kind of fun," he replies, touching my hand.

"Alright, last question. What is your favorite form or body of water and three deep reasons why? When I say form of water, I'm meaning it could be like ice or rain, or it could be a body of water, like a waterfall or jacuzzi or specific place," I explain.

Matteo doesn't hesitate with this question, "Lake Atitlan. That's my favorite body of water. It's the most beautiful volcanic lake."

"Oh I love volcanoes! I've never seen one in person but hope to one day," I interject.

"Maybe we could go sometime," he says with a smile. My face turns red and I just smile.

"It is just a magical place. I went there in my mid 20s and it felt magical, like it was meant for me. Another reason I love it is because it was freeing, it was freedom. Another reason is that it helped foster my individuality. When I was there, nothing else mattered. I felt like everyone that was there was supposed to be there at that time. We had a special bond. The people were all from different walks of life but somehow were together at that time, it felt unique and meant to be."

"Love those answers!" I say, "Ok, this is what they tell me about you." Matteo looks at me, anticipating my next words.

"Alright, your favorite color represents the truth about how you see yourself, how you view your own personality. You mentioned warm, energizing, calming, and life-giving, right?"

"Wow, that's really cool," he says, taking it all in.

"Would you say those things are true for you? How you see yourself?" I ask.

"Yes, I think so. I don't always take the time to think about myself and how I come off to people, but I'm glad I think about myself that way, I think it's positive," he says, to which I confirm.

"For the favorite animal, this represents the truth about what you want in an ideal life partner," I say with a smirk. "So let's revisit. You would like companionship, someone to be there when you get home, someone that you can take care of, someone with a great smile," I say as he is blushing and nodding in agreement.

"And for the final question about water, this represents the truth about your view of your own sexuality, your attitude towards sex, which can also be viewed as your approach towards life itself," I explain, watching him take in this information.

"What did I say about that one?" he asks.

"See, isn't it a good thing I wrote it down?" I say with a laugh. "Ok, your view or attitude toward sex...from what you mentioned, you feel that it's magical, special, meant to be. It has helped you individuate yourself in life, you also see it as freeing. So maybe sex makes you feel free, but also bonds you, does that sound right?"

"Yes! That's so interesting. Wow. How is it connected to how I see life itself?"

"I think that how you approach sex can explain how you approach life. People that are uncomfortable or hesitant with sex may be risk averse in life, ya know? I just thought of that as an example, I'm not 100% that it's true," I explain.

"It makes a lot of sense though," Matteo says. I can tell that he is really thinking about this. "It's a lot to reflect on. You are so smart, by the way, and it's incredibly sexy," he says as I am filled with embarrassment. "I have never had a date like this, so introspective and unique."

I get uncomfortable with the compliment and blush as I say, "Thank you. Thank you for indulging me."

"Wait, what were your answers?" he asks.

"Let me grab them," I rummage around in my oversized bag until I find the paper with my scribbled answers. "So, my favorite color is blue. Blue feels incredibly calming to me, no matter what shade it is. It's a color that represents expansion to me, it's an infinite color. I love how it's reflected in our Earth; the sky above is blue, the depths of the ocean are shades of dark blue. It reminds me of this ancient quote, I think it's in the Emerald Tablet, I can't remember who said it, but it's, 'as above, so below.' It means something like the microcosm and the macrocosm and how both affect each other. Like, the sun impacts the changing of seasons, and the moon affects the tides of the water—'as above, so below.' Basically we are all interconnected and that's how blue makes me feel. Wow, that was long winded, sorry."

"No, I love it! So you see yourself as calming and infinite, impacting others. I feel like this correlates to the work you do," he says, another compliment I try to take in.

"That's really kind," I say.

"It's what you are! It tracks," he says, smiling.

"For my favorite animal, ugh, I know I initially liked dog, but I put down a fox, and now I'm realizing that isn't a good thing, possibly," I explain.

"Oooo, a fox?" he says with a laugh. "Tell me more."

"I wrote that a fox is clever, very intelligent, they are mysterious and sneaky, but beautiful, almost dog-like," I say, judging myself. "This isn't good, I need to work on this because I don't want a partner that is sneaky or mysterious, I really want and need transparency."

"It's ok, I think that it shows you want something exciting. And, you said dog-like, so you want those companionship type qualities," he says.

"True, I feel like I still hear some of my desire for a bad boy, still trying to unlearn that one," I say with a laugh. I can tell Matteo is thinking something about this comment but I'm not sure what.

"I think it's just liking some mystery or excitement," he says and I can tell he's trying to make me feel better.

"Alright, last one. For the water, I know this sounds lame, but I put down a really warm swimming pool or jacuzzi. When I get in a pool, I instantly feel a release," I stop and laugh. "Wow, this is quite literal for how I view sex." Matteo laughs out loud.

"I have a dirty mind, I guess. I also put down that it's soothing and makes me feel sexy and I can be naked?" I say, surprising myself with my answers. "Wow, I am surprising myself, I don't even consider myself that sexual."

"It's your subconscious though, right? So, maybe it's something you just have to get more tapped into," he says, holding my gaze.

"Maybe," I say with a smile.

A moment later, Matteo begins to touch my legs that are crossed before pulling me quickly from the other side of the couch.

"Come over here, I want to be close to you," he says as he places a pillow behind my head so that I'm comfortable. My heart pounds in my chest, each beat louder than the last. The touch is light, almost tentative, but it sends a shiver down my spine. His hand slips to the back of my neck, gentle but insistent, guiding me toward him. Our lips meet, softly at first, as if testing the waters. But then the kiss deepens, a slow burn that ignites something inside me. It's as if the world around us fades away, all my exhaustion, worries, and fears, leaving just the two of us, locked in this moment. The warmth of his breath, the taste of his lips, the way his hand tightens just slightly in my hair—it's all consuming.

4/23/24

STATUS

"There is no greater agony than bearing an untold story inside you." —Maya Angelou

"What's your marital status?" the nurse asks, fingers poised over her keyboard.

"Umm, going through a divorce," I lie. I can feel heat coming over my body.

"Ok, so should I mark you down as separated or married?" she infers.

"Separated," I reply automatically, barely thinking. She types it in without looking up, already moving on to the next question.

My mouth goes dry. **Separated?** Why did I say that? It's not true. I'm divorced. The word tastes wrong, like I've betrayed myself. I sit there, frozen, replaying the conversation. She's already halfway through the rest of her questions, and the window to correct myself has closed.

"I don't want to even say separated. I am DIVORCED. I am supposed to be free. Why didn't I follow up on the divorce decree? But I'm so fucking

sick of being the responsible one. I'm so fucking over it!" I scream inside my head.

After the divorce was finalized, my lawyer sent Tripp an email instructing him to remove me from the health insurance plan within 30 days. She encouraged me to begin looking at health plans for myself immediately. "Yeah, okay, I'll get right on that," I responded sarcastically. I had just endured a two year long divorce, I needed a break from maneuvering and paperwork. I was burnt out after so much seemingly endless advocating and fighting. One more task felt impossible.

A month went by. Then another. Then another. Life got busy and I didn't follow up on it, I wasn't seeing any doctors anyway. But then, weird things started happening with my health.

Jude's bathtub clogged with enough of my hair to fill a doll's wig, debilitating cramps that brought me to my knees, the creeping sense of unease as I googled every symptom I had. I knew I needed to see a doctor. But the cost of health insurance was something I just did not have it in me to deal with.

Everyone said the same thing: my friends, my therapist. "It's not your fault. You can't afford your own plan, so what's the harm? If he hasn't submitted the decree, that's on him." And most of the time, I believed them. During the day, I could almost convince myself they're right. But at night, when the house got quiet, unease slipped in like a draft.

What if he finds out? What if this becomes another weapon in his arsenal, another thing he throws in my face? I'm supposed to be untangling myself from him. I'm supposed to be free. But this feels like a tether I can't quite cut.

The nurse's voice brings me back to the present. "Okay, you're all set. Head to room three."

I nod, gripping my bag as I walk down the hall. But in my head, I'm still turning the word over and over: **Separated.** The shame clings like static.

I shouldn't have to fight this hard to claim what I already know is true: **I am divorced. I deserve to feel free.**

4/26/24

SURGERY

"There in all this cold and hollow world, no fount of deep, strong, deathless love; save that within a mother's heart" ~ Felicia Hemans

It's a cozy Saturday night. My mom is staying with me for Jude's upcoming surgery on Monday. I'm relieved that she's here. It feels nice to have someone around to help me with Jude as I prep for the upcoming weeks. I have no idea how he'll respond to the surgery and I'm praying it will go smoothly.

My mom and I are sorting Jude's clothes, setting aside his baggiest mesh shorts that will give him plenty of space while he is healing, when I hear a "ding" coming from my phone. I glance over to see who is texting me.

"It's Tripp," I say and my mom looks at me with concern.

"Are you going to check it??" she asks almost frantically.

"I will check it when we are finished," I say in a tone to remind her that we are on our time, not his. Any type of contact from him evokes a sense of urgency. My mom still gets anxious when she hears a police siren and I feel responsible for that. I still hold so much guilt that she had to be there that infamous day when the cops were called. My mind will sometimes take me right back to the moment too. I can feel myself crouching behind the neighbor's trees, hoping the police arrive before he finds us. All it takes is a particular smell of summertime fresh cut grass and I'm right back there, my body trembling in fear.

"I am against the surgery," the text reads.

I want to rage. How dare he try to sabotage the surgery or think that his input matters when it's given at the last minute. He's had weeks to discuss this.

"This is the first time I'm hearing that. I said I'd leave it in your court to discuss further, but you haven't attempted to be involved," I respond.

I put down my phone, anticipating that he'll be writing paragraphs to me. I focus on tasks to get finished before Monday and enjoy time watching Trad Wives on YouTube with my mom.

Before I fall asleep, I quickly glance at my messages. He never responded. *"Good,"* I think, still surprised he didn't write more.

"WHAT TIME IS HIS PROCEDURE?" Tripp asks at 9:58 am on the day of Jude's surgery.

"It's at 11. He's about to go back," I reply along with a picture of Jude lying sweetly on the hospital gurney in the same hospital gown that he had at his 14-week-old surgery. It is a light spring green color covered with cartoon drawings of little tigers sleeping in different positions with little leaves and "zzzs" dotted throughout. In soft pencil writing, it says "tired little tiger" all over it. The sight of the smock brings tears to my eyes.

"Please tell him I love him," he replies.

"Jude, Daddy just wrote me and he says he loves you very much!" I say to him. He does a little side smile and continues to bounce around. My mom gives me a silent, disapproving look. I can tell she's both angry and heartbroken that Tripp isn't involved.

"We're going to the pool!" Jude says enthusiastically.

"I know it kind of looks and smells like the pool, but it's the hospital, baby," I say, hoping he understands. I don't want him to associate the YMCA with hospitals since we both love swimming.

THE SURGERY IS CURRENTLY in progress and to distract us both from our anxiety, my mom and I load up on comfort food from the hospital dining hall for emotional support. We get loaded mashed potatoes, with extra cheese and sour cream, two large Cokes, Bavarian pretzels with cheese, and two donuts, one for us to split and the other for Jude.

Just as we are polishing off the final disgusting bits of food, we catch a glimpse of the doctor heading our way. I perk up and mouth, "Everything okay?" The doctor smiles and gives a thumbs up. My mom and I look to each other relieved.

"Everything went great! The surgery took not quite 20 minutes and he's in recovery now. The foreskin was extremely tight. I can bet that he will be feeling much better after he's healed. I put a really good amount of surgical glue around the stitches, so he will be comfortable. The stitches will dissolve in about a week. Just make sure to follow the instructions for Tylenol and Ibuprofen to keep him comfortable," the doctor explains.

"Thank you so so much for everything," I reply.

"Yes, we are so grateful for you!" my mom shares.

"You are so welcome. Please reach out if anything is needed, but otherwise, they'll be out shortly to bring you back to recovery. You both take care," she says, then heads to the OR.

My mom and I look at each other and sigh out of relief at the exact same time. We both let our bodies collapse into the benches and talk over what the doctor said.

Just then, my phone dings.

"Does he have to go under for the procedure? Maybe we can chat a minute shortly? I won't be negative at all—just worried about him" Tripp writes.

"He's done already. Just talked to the doctor. He's waking up now but it will be a few before I can go back. Free if you want to talk," I reply.

"Call you in one minute," he responds.

My mom looks at me.

"You sure you should talk with him?" she asks, skeptical.

"It's fine. It's about Jude's health and he wants to know. It's a good sign if he finally wants to know. He should want to know, it's ridiculous he hasn't even tried to talk to the doctor, but he's never been able to handle medical things," I say.

"No, he never has been able to. Being a parent is hard but you have to set your own stuff aside to do what is best for them," my mom says.

"You are preaching to the choir, mom."

"I know," she says, stirring the ice in her cup around before letting out a sad, disappointing sigh. I sigh too.

"I KNOW it's late for me to be calling and I don't want to argue, I just...I'm not good with these things," he says.

"I know," I respond.

"I'm working on it, I just don't want him to have to deal with pain."

"Tripp, it was either now or in the future. It would be more challenging if he didn't do it," I explain.

"Did they have to cut the whole thing or just a little?" he asks.

I explain the whole issue again, for the second time. I focus on my breathing to keep myself calm because I want to scream. I have to remember what Celeste said; he has wet brain from the drug use.

"Well, you are a really good mom and it makes me feel good that he's well taken care of," he says. I want to snap back at him and sarcastically say, "I'm so glad I get to be of service to you and make being an absent parent so easy for you!" But I don't.

"Thank you," I reply, then hang up the call.

I walk back to the table where my mom is texting someone, probably my dad or my sister, telling them that Tripp finally contacted me and how ridiculous it is since the surgery was already completed.

"So how did that go? It's in true Tripp fashion, always after the fact," she says then takes a sip from her fountain drink.

"He wanted to know how much they would cut...and to tell me I'm a good mom," I recap.

My mom rolls her eyes then after a couple moments, seems sad... then she begins to cry.

"Mom, what's wrong??" I plead.

"I just can't believe him. Jude is so perfect and precious; I don't know how he can go a day without him. I don't know how he got so off course. I'll never understand it. How can he live like this? Take the marriage out of it, how can he live everyday without seeing his son? Why hasn't he done everything he possibly could to get better?"

Tears start streaming down my face, not because I'm consciously grieving, but because my mom's tears have cracked me open. It hits me—I haven't really let myself cry. I've been holding it all in, refusing to feel the loss that lingers in my bones. I've kept it locked away, terrified that if I let it out, the pain will be unbearable. We talk it over, my mom and I, like we always do, trying to wrap the hurt in words and reason. We come to the same conclusion we always do: everything has worked out the way it was supposed to, and now it's up to him to make it different. But even that doesn't bring comfort—it's truth, but it doesn't make the reality any less painful.

The hospital attendant enters the waiting room, calling our names. My heart skips a beat. We walk down a long, sterile hallway. With each step, the anticipation builds, and all I can think about is getting to my baby boy. Finally, after what feels like an eternity, we reach his room.

There he is—my sweet boy, lying in that too-big hospital bed, his tender face peaceful in sleep. Relief washes over me like a tidal wave, but it's tinged with something deeper, something raw. I move toward him, and as I do, all the fear, the worry, the helplessness I've kept buried, all of it rises to the surface. I can't hold back anymore. I crawl into the bed beside him, careful not to disturb him, and cuddle up close, breathing in his precious scent—the scent of home, of love, of everything that matters.

"Thank you, God. Thank you, Universe. Thank you, my angels. Thank you," I whisper, the words spilling out like a prayer, a plea, and a promise, all at once. The tears keep coming, but now they're tears of gratitude, of overwhelming love. I press my cheek against his, feeling the warmth of his skin, and I know, I would do anything for this little boy. I would go through every fear, every pain, every sleepless night a thousand times over just to keep him safe, to hold him like this.

As I lay here, wrapped around my son, I realize that this is what it means to love with your whole heart. It's not just the joy, the pride, the laughter. It's the ache, the fear, the vulnerability. It's letting yourself feel it all, even when it hurts, even when you're scared to death, because that's what makes it real. This is my boy. And he is everything.

5/5/24

NOT MY PROBLEM

"For a moment, the whole world seemed to hold its breath." ~ Baroness Orczy

"Have you been giving him money?" I ask John, cutting straight to the point. John is one of Tripp's friends from way back—those days when they both waited tables at a fancy New York City restaurant. Now, John's moved on to Wall Street, while Tripp's been drifting through the film industry.

"I haven't been giving him money, no," John replies, almost defensively. "But I am letting him stay at my other apartment for free."

And just like that, everything falls into place. I remember Google mapping Tripp's new address from some court documents a few months ago, and was surprised to find it was an apartment overlooking Central Park.

My mind drifts back to a time when we used to daydream about the perfect place to live. I always pictured a big white house with a wraparound porch, grasses swaying in salt air, a beach or lake just steps away. Tripp's dream was different—a large, beautiful brownstone overlooking Central Park. I guess he got his wish.

"Wait, let me get this straight," I say, my voice rising. "He's almost two months behind on child support, hasn't sent his share for childcare this month, and yet he's living in that apartment for free? The one you used to rent out on Airbnb?"

"Yes, it's my investment property," John answers, a bit too casually. "I'm sorry to hear he hasn't paid up. I know things have been slow work-wise—the writer's strike really hit his industry hard. I've even been helping him look into jobs, like waiting tables again."

I feel something inside me snap.

"Let me see if I understand this correctly," I say, struggling to keep my voice steady. "I'm here in Ohio, barely making ends meet, seriously considering signing up for Sugar Babies just to keep the lights on, running a private practice by day and caring for Jude by night—getting him to his speech and OT appointments—while Tripp lounges in NYC, living for free and not working? If he really cared about his child, he'd have gotten a job—hell, he could bartend if he wasn't so delusional about his supposed sobriety. Giving him everything for free doesn't help him. He hasn't hit rock bottom yet."

My words come out sharper than intended, but they're the truth. "He's not my problem anymore, John. I'm not his wife anymore. I moved all the way to Ohio to escape this chaos, and he's still finding ways to disrupt my peace."

John shifts uncomfortably. "I don't think you understand. His friends are afraid he might hurt himself—he's been sounding suicidal."

A familiar wave of anger rises in me. "Yes, I do understand," I say, my voice ice cold. "He's pulled this before. He's not only acted out in ways that have hinted at this—he's threatened me with it. Told me he'd end his life if I left, if he ever lost me or Jude. And guess what? He's still alive."

I can't help but laugh bitterly, realizing how much I sound like Alanis Morissette in "You Oughta Know." It's almost poetic. Just like

Alanis, I'm here to remind Tripp—and everyone enabling him—of the mess he left when he blew up our lives.

"I'm not trying to be insensitive, John, but threatening suicide can be just another way to manipulate. I want him to get better—for his sake, for Jude—but I can't sacrifice my own mental health anymore. Jude has one healthy parent, and I can't let the other unhealthy one drag me down. Everyone's so focused on helping *him*. What about *me*?"

My voice cracks as I try to hold back tears. "During the divorce, Tripp had to present a statement of net worth, and it was full of people who've loaned him money. Everyone rushes to his aid after hearing his sob story, but no one thinks about what I'm going through—the one actually caring for the child! I'm dealing with my own health issues, and I just can't take on any more stress. This might sound harsh, but I have to set a firm boundary now."

John listens, and I can feel him understanding. "I get it," he says softly. "I don't want you to ever feel like you have to do something like joining Sugar Babies. I know you're the one caring for Jude, and I care about all three of you. If you're ever struggling financially, please, don't hesitate to reach out."

His offer surprises me, and for a moment, I feel a wave of embarrassment for losing it on him.

"Thank you," I say, tears spilling over. "I'm sorry for getting so upset, for unloading all this on you. It's just…it's so hard. I don't want to take help from anyone; I don't want to be indebted anymore, but just hearing your offer means so much."

"You don't need to apologize," John reassures me. "It sounds incredibly stressful, and I'm so sorry for what you've been through. I'm really glad we had this conversation—it's made a lot of things make sense, given what Tripp has told me."

"I've worried people don't know the full story," I admit, "that he's omitting parts to fit his narrative. But I've had to let go of worrying about what others think, because I know my own truth. I'm not trying to alienate him from his son; I want him to be a father, to get it together. I still deeply love and miss the person he was before the drugs and alcohol took over. It's incredibly painful."

"I'm so sorry," John says again, his voice filled with genuine sympathy. "I really think he's trying to get on the right path, to make things right. I'll only reach out if it's something you really need to know about, okay?"

"Thank you," I reply, feeling a small sense of relief. "Thank you for being a good friend to him. I really hope he can make it work this time."

A few days later, Tripp texts me to say he's been in the hospital. He had an adverse reaction to his new medication, which was affecting his thinking. He says he's getting better, that he wants to rebuild, to become the best co-parents we can be for Jude. I'm relieved to read his words, even though I'm holding my breath.

5/15/24

NOT MYSELF

"The heart will break, but broken live on" ~ Lord George Gordon Byron

"I don't feel like myself, something is wrong with me," I say to the gyno— specifically the second gyno that I have seen in the past month, this one for a second opinion after the first came up with no explanation for my symptoms. Hoping she will have an answer, I continue, "I have never felt exhaustion like this before, it's almost like I can't keep my eyes open in the morning and I've never been like this."

"What other symptoms are you experiencing?" she asks while typing on her computer.

"In March, I noticed I had a noticeable hump on the back of my neck, like a fat pad between my shoulders, then tons of my hair started falling out, not just a little, like a whole brush full every time. I gained over 20 lbs in a few months without changing my diet. I did go off of birth control in December and never had a period for months. But since April, I've been having extremely light bleeding every single day. I feel like I am on my period every day, which is miserable, ya know? Oh, they also found a large cyst on my left ovary with a 'daughter cyst' inside it, so weird," I say.

"Any changes in your life?" the gyno asks again, still not looking up from the computer, but I can still feel she is actively listening and invested as I begin to laugh.

"Oh yea, where do I begin? Moved to Ohio mid December from NY with my son. The judge signed off on it so you know there must have been issues for me to be able to move out of state," I say sarcastically while simultaneously cringing at the truth. "I finally got divorced in March and I am officially a single mom."

"How's your son?" she asks.

"Oh, he's doing great! He is autistic and has a speech delay, he's made so much improvement lately with it. I really think the tension in the household affected him more than I realized," I say as a horrible wave of grief and guilt wash over me and I begin to hold back tears. My chin begins to move, twisting and dimpling until I just let a sob out into my hands.

The gyno gets up swiftly and hands me a few tissues. She sits down on the nearby swivel chair and looks at me, kindly.

"What you are describing to me sounds like you've been in a depressive episode. I'm not surprised; you have been through so much. Your body is adjusting to the changes; you have a different level of stress than other parents since you are caring for a child with a disability on your own."

As she spoke, I began to feel a release, then surprise. How could I have missed this? I was so focused on my physical symptoms that I never considered they were connected to the stress. I often educate people on things, exactly like this, being psychosomatic, and here I was, surprised by the mention of it.

"Are you in therapy?" she asks.

"Yes, and I have a psychiatrist. She had me on 150mg of Zoloft during the divorce and I thought I was better so she agreed to begin to slowly wean me off of it," I explain.

"When was that?" she asks.

"Hmm, late April I believe. I've dealt with depression on and off my whole life and it's never been like this, I've never had the exhaustion like this so I really think it has to be physical," I say, making sure that she understands this can't be boiled down to depression.

"You've likely never had stressors like these before either," she says, holding my gaze. I look away and shake my head.

"I don't want to take medicine anymore, I don't want this whole experience holding me back," I reply. "Is this because I scored high on the PHQ-9? I could feel your assistant's concern when answering, but trust me, I want to live," I say sarcastically. PHQ-9 is the Patient Health Questionnaire that is typically given at doctor's appointments to assess depression and suicidality.

"Believe me, I've been there. When I went through my divorce, I lost so much hair that I had to clip the front part of my hair back into a little pouf in the front like something from the '80s, it definitely did not look good, but it hid a big bald spot," she shared with me, easing my defensiveness, "I had to be put on both Zoloft and Cymbalta for two years so that I could work, it was a terrible time."

I listened intently, realizing I can't control the way that the stress manifests and for how long it will persist.

"Sometimes, we get even more perspective after events like these. Maybe you hadn't experienced a true depressive episode until this, ya know?" she says, turning back to her computer and typing away. "I want to do another follow-up ultrasound in four weeks to check on the growth of the cysts, and I recommend that you meet with your psychiatrist to adjust your medication. Take the birth control the other gynecologist prescribed because it will hopefully keep the cyst from growing, but we will get confirmation at the next visit."

I nod, but inside, I feel that familiar churn of frustration. Birth control. The same medication I stopped because I'm already managing enough meds and remember, I don't have fallopian tubes. They're gone. Removed in a surgery I agreed to because my ex-husband was too scared to go under the knife himself and because getting pregnant again would've been dangerous for me.

But birth control can help shrink cysts, and I'm tired of fighting. So I nod again, agreeing just to move the conversation along. Sometimes, it's easier to go with the flow, even if the flow feels a little unfair.

THE ELEVATOR STOPS at the first floor of the hospital and as I'm walking out I find my dad waiting for me in the lobby. He offered to drive me to the gyno appointment since I'd been experiencing dizzy spells. Initially, I rejected his offer but quickly reconsidered as a wave of nausea came over me. I could tell he was concerned about me even though he didn't say it. I like this side of my dad.

A few minutes into the drive home, he breaks the silence.

"So, did this doctor give you any answers?" he asks.

"We are doing a follow up ultrasound for the cyst, but she basically thinks I've been in a depressive episode," I say calmly.

He takes a moment to respond. I can tell by his expression that he's trying to process this information.

"Do you feel like you are?" he asks.

"On one hand, I feel like it's an easy explanation, but I do see the signs. I'm going to meet with my psychiatrist and discuss increasing my dosage," I reply. He nods his head and we sit silently until finally approaching my exit.

"It does run in our family," he says while I nod. It doesn't necessarily make me feel better but he's trying.

We finally get home and I recap the visit to my mother. She's incredibly relieved that it isn't something "worse." She plops down on the couch and lets out an audible exhale of relief. I feel confused. Yes, I'm glad that I am physically healthy for the most part, but if this is all mental, this is scary. If this is depression and my medication is the issue, I will never stop taking my medication. Ever. I never want to go through this again.

Later that night, I talk to my friend Lisa and she is skeptical of what the gyno said. I am too, knowing that doctors often downplay women's health concerns, but there is a part of me that is genuinely curious to see if I'll feel better once the medication is increased.

5/19/24

THE EXCHANGE

"Trust, but be cautious whom you trust." ~ Publilius Syrus,

Ohio's skies, endless and gray, seem to stretch out like the monotony of my days. Since settling into the unhurried rhythm of this place, I've felt a numbness creeping in, an apathy that wraps around me like a too-worn sweater. I'm trying to date, trying to care, but it's hard when life feels so flat.

Dating has become a frustrating exercise in patience. Matteo is different, though. I like him, like *really* like him, but everything between us is moving at a glacial pace—slower than a snail's crawl, and it's driving me mad. I find myself daydreaming about escaping to his place in Cincinnati, where we could sip red wine from those elegant glasses he had made in Denmark, laughing and getting lost in each other's eyes. More than anything, I want to be with a man who embraces fatherhood, who loves it as much as he loves the idea of us. I crave that connection, that warmth, but I can't understand why he isn't trying to lock down a date the way I'm aching to with him.

Sunday, May 19th

ME: *I'm trying to finalize plans with some friends for this weekend and want to prioritize seeing you. It's Memorial Day weekend so I wasn't sure if you had set plans yet. Let me know your thoughts when you have time. Night!*

It's Tuesday night and no text back from Matteo. He's never been great about texting since the beginning, but this isn't feeling good. It is starting to make me feel bad about myself so I go on Hinge.

Once I'm in the app, I flip through a couple profiles then go to my inbox. I scroll down and find my first crazy messages with Matteo. I read through it and my heart fills up. I like him so much. I want to look at his pictures so I click on his profile. I scroll down and notice that something has changed...his location.

I sit up, staring at the screen. It no longer says Cincinnati...it says "Downtown Atlanta."

WTF.

I immediately ring Remy.

"His location changed to Atlanta! I know he's there for a conference and we aren't exclusive, but he can barely make time for me BUT he can make time for Hinge?!" I shout into the phone. Due to the past infidelity, I am not sure if my rage is legitimate. I really don't know if I'm thinking clearly, but all I know is that I'm piiissseeeddd. It doesn't help that I've been bleeding everyday and feeling like I'm on my period. It all makes me feel out of control. I don't want to feel this way anymore, I can't take it.

"Trust your gut. You have been feeling strung along for a while and he hasn't been making the time. It isn't okay, but you should give him a chance to give an explanation," Remy says calmly.

We hang up and I decide that I'm done. I don't care what his reasoning is for it, this isn't working for me. He is either fully in or he's out and that's all there is to it.

Wednesday, May 22nd

MATTEO (finally): *Traveling these past couple weeks has been exhausting! I've been in Florida and Atlanta since Sunday, waking up early and going to bed late.*

I'm at this fancy event right now at the Atlanta Aquarium.

I'm sorry for not responding sooner for this weekend! Things have been a bit up in the air. It looks like I'm going to be in Atlanta through Sunday and then I'll have my girls on Monday. Sorry! I would like to see you sooner than later!

What plans have you been thinking about doing with your friends this weekend?

I'm fuming inside. I'm being strung along. My mind begins to race. Why would he need to stay in Atlanta until Sunday? He's not working through the weekend, he has been setting up dates. "Things have been up in the air?" Sure they have, your dick has been up in the air and in someone else! I can't trust men, they are never honest. Never!

I want to make him sweat, so I don't respond right away. I will gather my thoughts and send them tomorrow. I don't want to feel this way. I hate the vulnerability of caring for someone. I'm not ready to have that pain again.

Thursday, May 23rd

ME: *Matteo, I care about you deeply, but I need to let you know where I'm at with our connection. I expressed my need for more communication and time together in hope that we could become folded into each other's lives more, but we are in contact so infrequently that the growing connection, that feels so strong when we talk/spend time together, seems to always plateau in between. I am very intentional about dating and I feel it's best for me to pursue a connection that is aligned with my needs and prioritized; I want us both to find what we want/deserve. I'm grateful for our* time together, but feel it's best for me to let this go. I'm open to a phone call or FaceTime if you want to discuss anything.

MATTEO: *I really appreciate your note, Meredith. I'm a bit surprised, but I do understand. I think you've caught me during the busiest few weeks I've had in a long time. Between starting a new job and traveling to these conferences, it has just been incredibly busy and I've barely had time to even check in with Clem & Rory. Despite all that, I want you to know that I'm very sorry that I haven't been able to give you what you want and deserve.*

I completely understand how we all have moments in time when we're incredibly busy and other moments where we need more from those we care about. At times when I wasn't working, I felt a similar way about us. Timing is so important for relationships, and part of what I'm hearing from you right now is that the timing between us just isn't right at the moment despite us caring for one another.

I understand that you've made up your mind and that you've put a lot of thought into your last message which I respect, but I'd still like to have a conversation with you, not to change your mind, but for us not to end things over text which can sometimes come across as cold and lead to misunderstandings. If I can sneak away from a conference session tomorrow I'll call you. If not, I'd really appreciate us connecting next week. <3

ME: *Thank you for responding and understanding. I do not want any misunderstandings and I'm sorry if this did feel out of the blue, so I want to be more transparent.*

I asked on Sunday about making plans for this weekend since scheduling childcare can be tough and I wanted to prioritize time with you. When I didn't hear from you on Tuesday, I reminded myself that you are super busy and that's likely why I didn't hear from you. By Wednesday morning, I started feeling a little sad and like an afterthought, like I was in a situationship. So, I got on Hinge, which I hadn't been on in months. After scrolling, I went back in my messages to read over our first convo. It made me happy. Then, I looked at your profile and your location was downtown Atlanta. While you were not able to write me back, you were able to change your location in Hinge. That stung. While we are not official and you can do whatever you like, I have been transparent about only dating you and I want to invest and date someone that knows they want me and only me. Given my history, you can understand how important that is.

I am very much open to discussing by phone bc I do very much care for you.

MATTEO: *Hi Meredith. I'm just now getting back to my hotel with my colleagues. Thank you for sharing what you wrote. Phew! That makes a lot more sense now.*

It's true, during the first social event at this conference I was chatting with a guy who recently got divorced. He asked about online dating so I showed him the app. At some point yesterday I remembered and switched it back to Cincinnati. Regardless, I'm really sorry that I hurt you! It was unintentional, but you don't deserve that as I care about you too. It means a lot that you shared what your train of thought was. Thank you.

Beyond that blooper of mine, I really appreciate you sharing your feelings and how this whole debacle made you feel. I know the cadence between us hasn't been great lately and that's entirely my fault and I'm sorry.

The reason why I think we should do a call together is because although I may not be able to give you what you want right now, I don't think it should mean that we should never talk again. Timing plays a big role in relationships, and I kinda feel that's the biggest barrier right now between us. I think talking about it will help us both understand one another better. <3

I don't know why, I just do not respond that night.

Friday, May 24th

MATTEO: *Hi. I'll have a break in ~30 minutes if you're available to chat. A session ends at 2:15 so I can call you around 2:20ish. I then have something at 3pm.*

If that doesn't work, I'd really like to find time next week for us.

ME: *Hi, yes let's chat then. Talk soon.*

Matteo calls me and I can hear commotion in the background, he's talking in a corner during a busy work conference. His voice is soothing and kind, he apologizes over and over. It's healing in some strange way, but I also don't want him doing it at the same time. Yet, I'm not sure if I totally believe him and I'm worried that my ex has damaged my view on men forever.

During the call, we realize that it isn't the right time. I want to have fun with him, like weekend getaways together and to start becoming something. He has this new job and increasing obligations. He wants me to live life and wants the door to stay open. I explain that I want the freedom to date and if it works later on, it works, and if not, we are both happy to know each other. We end the call like friends, mature adults. It's new, it's strange, I'm not sure how I feel about it.

Saturday, May 25th

MATTEO: *Hi. I know our chat wasn't easy, but I'm really happy we had it. I care about you and want you to be happy.*

I'm super excited to hear about all that business news you shared at the end of the call!! You're building your own empire and I wanna continue to be your biggest fan! Love it!!

ME: *Thank you! I feel your support and I'm grateful I have you for the business guidance; it made a world of difference in the negotiating.*

I'm glad we had the convo too. I care about you so much and I don't want you out of my life. I would like to talk and spend time in person at some point when you have time. I don't want you to go away.

Matteo: That really means a lot. Thank you!

6/1/24

ROCKS & RAGE

"Trust thyself: every heart vibrates to that iron string." – Ralph Waldo Emerson

My phone begins to buzz and "Jude's Daddy" comes across my screen. *"Why is he calling me?"* I think to myself.

"I need to talk to you about something really important. I can text it if you prefer," he texts to me. The urgency worries me. Because of the protection order, we don't talk on the phone and only communicate through text regarding FaceTime and expenses related to Jude. Even though Jude is safe playing in the other room with the babysitter, I fear there is something going on that would affect him so I call him back.

"Hi," he says.

"Hi," I reply. There's tension and weirdness already. "What's going on?" I ask.

"Yea, so, I was looking through the health insurance statements and it looks like you've been to a lot of visits lately," he says not with concern, but more like curiosity.

"Mhmm," I reply. I wonder where he is going with this, surprised that he even checked anything medical since he avoided anything and everything related to the divorce, child support, and even restrictions related to the protection order.

"Do you know what I'm supposed to do about removing you?" he asks.

Fuck. Fuck. Fuck.

"You should go back and read the email my lawyer sent you. She notified you of the instructions and sent me a bill for doing so," I reply to him in an admittedly icy tone.

"I just need to know what to do because I don't think you can still be on it," he states innocently.

"I'm not making you keep me on it," I reply, icy again.

"Look, I was thinking, I'm happy to keep you on for 20 years and not report it. If I do that though, I need you to chill with the child support texts," he says.

Rage. Red-hot boiling rage fills my body and I try with everything in my being to stay calm.

"Absolutely not. Just remove me," I reply firmly.

"I'm not saying this to be a jerk, I'm really fine with keeping you on the health insurance. You've just been insistent on child support and I've been having a hard time finding work," he says.

The motherfucking audacity.

"You've been struggling to find work? I've been struggling to even work at all and manage raising a kid by myself," I say as my voice begins to rise.

"I think we should talk about this another time, I'm still very codependent with you and it's hard when you are upset with me," he replies.

This man is confused. What fucking therapist has he been going to? Codependent with me? Is that what is going on here? Or is it a man child that wants to bargain away supporting his child? I think the latter.

"Take me off the insurance, I wont have you holding this over my head. They are two separate issues. Child support is not negotiable and you are lucky that I haven't reported you for being behind in payments and had your checks garnished already," I reply. In this moment, I want to murder.

"It's clear you are not capable of having a calm conversation, so I am going to hang up now, bye," he says before I hear the click of the phone call ending.

I am taken right back to my old self, my worn down, angry self from during the divorce. I want to break everything in front of me but I can't. I can't hold it in, I can't take it! Luckily, the babysitter arrives right then and I know I have 30 minutes to think about how I get away from this motherfucker.

I burst outside, my steps quickening despite the oppressive July heat. I sprint down the bike path with a fierce determination, seeking distance from the houses and people. I find myself under a massive bridge, its concrete pillars and steel beams casting long shadows. The roar of traffic above is relentless.

Standing in the cool, dark underbelly of the bridge, I let out a primal scream. "AHHHHHHHH FUCK YOU! FUCK YOU! FUCK YOUU-UUUU!" The sound reverberates off the walls, my voice swallowed by the thunderous rumble of cars speeding above. The bridge trembles slightly with each passing vehicle, and my screams mix with the clamor.

"I CAN NEVER CATCH A BREAK, I CAN NEVER CATCH A FUCKING BREAAKKKKKKK. WHEN WILL IT END? FUCKKKKKKKKKKKKKK!"

I snatch up a rock, hurling it towards the creek below. It clatters against the dirt before rolling away, failing to make it to the water. I scoff at my miss and grab another rock, throwing it with all my might. This time, it lands with a satisfying splash. The rock's splash sends a shimmering ripple across the creek's surface. It's a small victory, a rare moment of perfect execution.

"That's fucking right!!!" I yell.

As the tension in my shoulders begins to dissolve, my jaw

unclenches, and my breathing steadies. The noise of the bridge and the roar of traffic start to fade into the background. My mind begins to clear. It's a lesson—yet again, I'm reminded of the need to break free.

I brush the dirt from my knees, finding solace in the cool, gritty ground. Standing up, I feel a wave of relief and clarity. I know I need to touch base with Celeste to ensure I'm navigating this correctly. I send her a text, and within moments, we set up a time to talk today.

"YOU'VE BEEN on my mind, how have you been?" Celeste asks enthusiastically.

"Oh, I've been good and bad. More good than bad. We'll get to me, tell me about you!" I say.

"Well, I'm pregnant—" I cut her off immediately.

"Pregnant? Congratulations!! I'm so happy for you!" I squeal!

"Thank you," she says kindly. "No one told me pregnancy was so hard on your body. It's been really tough."

"Oh, I know, it's awful. Have you had morning sickness?" I ask.

"I've had all day sickness. Bad nausea but no actual puking."

"It's so bad. I don't even know how I worked during that time," I reply.

"I know, I am really not sure how I'm going to be able to manage a child and work when I can barely work while pregnant," she shares. I am lucky to have a deeper glimpse into her life and challenges given that she witnessed so much of mine when she was my attorney. We continue to discuss motherhood and all that comes with it until she says, "Ok, now what's going on?"

"Oh Celeste," I begin, "you're gonna be upset with me, but I didn't get off the health insurance. I saw some doctors, and now Tripp is trying to bargain with me. He is saying he'll keep me on the insurance if I lay off him regarding child support."

There is no judgment in her voice as she instructs me that I must have him submit the divorce decree and if he wont, I'll need to contact them. She prepares me that I will likely have to pay back whatever the full cost of those visits were. She says that most hospitals will work out a payment plan. While she agrees that insurance is a scam, she says that they will never pay for something I wasn't covered for and that I need to get that freedom from Tripp. It isn't worth it, and I know she is right. My mind is made.

"IT'S STRANGE," I tell my psychiatrist, leaning back in the chair. "I didn't need coffee immediately this morning to keep my eyes open for the first time in forever. I guess it was partly depression."

"This is a good sign. You're responding to the medication," she says with a warmth that makes me feel seen.

"I suppose." I nod but can't shake the confusion. "But why didn't this happen before when I cut down on Zoloft? I've weaned off it so many times in my life."

She pauses, her eyes steady on mine. "I think it's important to consider the severity of your life circumstances this time. You are dealing with a lot more."

"Yeah, that's what the last gyno kept telling me too," I say, almost in resignation. Why did I care so much that I couldn't do it this time? What was I trying to prove to myself?

Reliance. The word sticks to me like a burr. I've spent my whole life avoiding it, determined to never rely on anyone again—because relying on people means being let down, eventually. But this time, Zoloft isn't letting me down; it's lifting me up. I was trapped in a dark, suffocating cave with no way out, and Zoloft was the ladder that has led me back to the light, back to myself.

At night, I dream of a room so dark it swallows everything. I know he is there—my ex, looming above me. I can feel his eyes on me, heavy and judgmental, as if they are burning into my skin. For what feels like hours, I stay still, not daring to move, pretending to be dead. If I make even the slightest movement, I fear he will stomp my head in, crush whatever is left of me.

But then, something changes. A sliver of light touches my cheek, warm and gentle. I hear voices—my voice—arguing with his; rising with strength I didn't know I still have. "Enough! Enough! Leave! You don't belong here. You've done enough!"

The words are a command, a final banishment. The door slams shut, and the silence that follows is a relief so profound it feels like an exhale after holding my breath for years.

I feel warmth spreading through me, like sunlight after a long winter. My own arms wrapped around me, pulling me into an embrace. "I love you," my voice whispers, soft and certain. "You can get up now." The warmth is so real, it soothes the deepest parts of my soul, and in this moment, I understand: I can rely on me.

7/1/24

WAS IT REAL?

"There is nothing more deceptive than an obvious fact." ~ Arthur Conan Doyle

It's the beginning of July and my parents are watching my son this weekend. I'm scrolling through videos on YouTube. Nothing is doing it for me. I turn it off. It's quiet and I'm alone with some chocolate, candies, popcorn, and my thoughts.

I think about Matteo and I still don't understand what happened. Did he even like me? Why can't I just let this go? My emotions have been all over the place and while I know that I am not exactly in the headspace, I impulsively send a voice memo.

"Hi Matteo, umm, I hope you are well. I'm alone tonight and just thinking about things. I just wanted to run something by you. Honestly, I just wanted to know if we really had something or if I made something up in my mind. Sometimes I don't trust my own memory, haha. So, if you don't mind, could you cross check this for me? Haha. Be well, bye!"

..."Oh. My. God. What did I just do??!" I shout out loud as I pace around the room, biting my nails. "I just made the most pathetic move of my life...or the smartest. I mean, who cares what he thinks of me?! But...I do care what he thinks of me. I want to know if I made this up! No, no, this is desperate. You don't need any understanding. It didn't work and that's that!"

I rush over to my bed and the voice note is marked as "Read." *Shit*. Maybe that just means that he's seen there's a voice note but hasn't actually listened yet.

I hold down my message until the text options come up and quickly click "delete." Done. I removed it.

Relief washes over me. I did it, it's fine. Crisis averted.

Then, my phone begins to ring.

Shit, it's him!

"Oh my gosh, hi Matteo!" I say sheepishly.

"It's so good to hear from you! I love hearing your voice!" he says enthusiastically.

"But Matteo, that voice note was all over the place. But please, you can be honest, or even harsh; was there actually something real between us? I just don't trust my memory," I say, anxiously awaiting his response.

"Oh course there was! I really think it was just timing. My work was ramping up, making things more difficult and you were finally having balance with childcare and more space for a relationship, and we had our misunderstanding. But yes, I have very deep feelings for you, that hasn't changed."

"You do? Then why don't you try to hang out more?" I ask honestly.

"I think I do need to be totally transparent and explain that. I don't know, you were just getting divorced and I was the first person you were dating after. I just have this feeling like you should date. As much as I'd love for you to be with me, I think I imagined in my mind that it would mean more if you dated around and a year later, you chose me."

I'm shocked by his words. On one hand, they are really romantic and understanding, and truly more of what I needed at the time than

I realized. On the other hand, I feel as if he took my decision and my choice about my readiness to enter a new relationship away from me.

"But Matteo, I have been dating. I explained that to you. I even dated during the divorce."

"I know, but there is like a second grieving period after the divorce. You anticipate this major thing finally ending and then once it's there, you are left with things to process you didn't anticipate," he explains.

I don't want to admit it, but he is right. My eagerness to see him was and is another form of escapism. I wanted to erase the pain and start a new life before I was actually ready.

Somehow, we shift into multiple topics, making for a phone call that lasts for over two hours. I feel so connected and in love with him. It is so easy and comfortable.

It's the next day, and Matteo texts me, thanking me for reaching out and expressing gratitude for our connection. I feel the same.

Oddly, I feel a shift happen inside, like I have permission to be alone with myself. Maybe I need to be bored here in Ohio for a while. Maybe I need to grieve. Maybe I am right where I need to be. I vow to myself that I will date if I feel like it but I will be alone with myself for another year. If he's the one, I'll know. If not, that's okay too.

7/13/24

SNAKES

"Anything you can imagine you can make real" ~ Jules Verne

I step out onto my back stoop, still marveling at the small miracles of this new life. A fenced-in yard, my own space. Coming from NYC, it feels like a dream. The grasses I planted are thriving in the June heat, their soft blue-green plumes swaying gently. As I take a seat, my gaze drifts downward, and there it is—a tiny snake skin, delicate and translucent, nestled among the grasses by my feet.

For a moment, I just stare. It feels almost sacred, like I've stumbled upon a secret the Universe has left for me to find. Something about its fragility, its weightlessness, moves me in a way that's hard to explain. People might think it's strange to tear up over a shed snake skin, but to me, it's proof of transformation. It's a tangible reminder that growth requires release, that we can't carry the old layers forever.

I lean back against the doorframe, a quiet, "Thank you," escaping my lips.

I truly feel like a snake. That might sound odd, given how often "snake" is used as an insult, a shorthand for deceit or betrayal. The Biblical snake gets blamed for introducing evil into the world, casting a shadow over the whole species. But I don't see it that way. If God created everything, then the snake must have its purpose too. Maybe the story of Adam and Eve isn't about punishment but about necessity. Lessons often come through discomfort, don't they? Snakes force us to look at what we'd rather not see—our limitations, our truths, our capacity for change.

I have felt throughout all of this like I was being *forced* to shed—to leave behind the marriage, the identity, the safety nets. But now, sitting here with this fragile skin at my feet, I realize it wasn't just something I had to endure. It was something that needed to happen.

Snakes, aside from literally growing out of their skin, also shed to remove parasites. Maybe that's also part of my purpose: extracting the parasitic parts of my old life—the toxicity, the self-doubt, the fear of being on my own. And let's be real—self-doubt is the sneakiest parasite of all. It doesn't announce itself like fear or toxicity. It doesn't walk in, throw its bags on the floor, and demand to be acknowledged. No, self-doubt is subtle, it makes small, almost imperceptible cuts. It sidles up, all charming and nonchalant, and whispers, *Are you sure you're good enough? Smart enough? Brave enough?* And self-doubt rarely starts with just you. It's planted, often by the people who are supposed to love you the most. Their words stick, making you stay in the corner, apologizing for taking up space. It wants you to shrink, to be small, to never dare. But shedding is the opposite of shrinking—it's messy, raw, and unapologetically expansive.

For so long, I was convinced I had to prune myself down to something easier to love, like a well-tended bonsai tree, instead of the wild, tangled forest I actually am. It's not Instagram-pretty, but it's showing all my parts because hiding isn't safety; it's suffocation. We're all walking around so terrified of being *too much*—too emotional, too human—that we've built these perfectly curated walls and expectations around ourselves. And then we wonder why we feel so disconnected, so anxious, so deeply, profoundly *stuck*. That's how depression pulls you under—by convincing you that it's safer to hide than to be fully seen.

Fuck anyone who tries to shame me (or you) for shedding. I've outgrown the version of me that made people comfortable, and I'm not going back. Snakes don't apologize for shedding. They don't worry about who's watching or how awkward they look mid-shed. They don't cling to their old skin or try to patch it up. They shed because they *have to*, because their growth demands it. And once they're free, they don't look back.

Without snakes, the ecosystem collapses. Without pain, we don't grow. Without shedding, we stay stuck. So, if shedding my old skin makes me even a little scary to some people? Good. I'm not here to be palatable. I'm here to grow.

And if the darkness is part of the deal, so be it. Depression, anxiety, fear—they're all trying to teach us something. They're signals that something isn't working, that we're clinging to an old life that no longer fits. The only way out is through.

So, if I'm a snake, good. I'll take it. The alternative? Shrinking myself, burying my light, contorting into something palatable just to make others comfortable? That's not life. That's a slow death. And I didn't survive all of this just to keep playing small.

I'm here to live.

7/24/24

SECRET STITCHING

"The beginning is the most important part of the work." ~ Plato

"Hey, Mere, do you stitch or do embroidery?" Carly texts. Carly's one of the friends I made in grad school, now running her own private practice here in Ohio. I've been wanting to connect more with her, yearning for a core group of friends in this city that still feels new to me. Maybe it's me, hesitating. Maybe it's her—four kids, a full-time practice. But she's reaching out, and that's great.

"Yes! Why?" I reply, probably a little too eagerly.

"I'm part of a secret sister stitching society," she says, her tone conspiratorial. "We make little embroidery pieces with empowering feminist images or statements and put them up around Columbus. I'd love for you to join. It's the first Tuesday of every month, and it's a blast. It's a mix of therapists you know and other women."

I nearly squeal. Finally, a chance to find my people here?

When I first moved back, I reached out to several people. Some I knew through friends, others from my past—like my best friend's childhood bestie with three kids, or the woman from college I'd once bonded with at a yoga retreat in Mexico. They were enthusiastic, but life got in the way. Meet-ups never materialized. I understood, of course. Families, marriages, and decades-old friendships—things I left behind in New York—don't just pause because someone new arrives in town.

I try not to feel sorry for myself, but it's hard making friends in a new city in your late 30s. Harder still when you don't quite feel like yourself but know deep down it's exactly what your mental health needs. I need women. Their laughter, their steady presence—something to tether me when my thoughts start spiraling.

"I'm so in! I know how to do embroidery, and I'd love to come!"

The stitching society meets at 7:30, just ten minutes from my house. I still marvel at how close everything is in Columbus compared to the sprawl of New York.

When I arrive at the building where Carly sees her clients, I'm instantly drawn to it, already dreaming of renting a space of my own again. The move, the finances—working from home felt necessary at first. But now, the constant time at home is suffocating. Maybe it's time for something different.

Carly greets me with a huge hug and shows me around her office, which is everything I'd want for myself. I catch myself imagining that, maybe one day, I could rent from her.

As we turn a corner, my heart skips a beat—Jackie! My friend from grad school, from the same clinical counseling program. It's like no time has passed. She looks and sounds exactly the same, down to her warm Canadian accent. We hug tightly.

"It's like seeing a long-lost friend!" I exclaim, a mix of joy and guilt bubbling up. *Why didn't I reach out when I moved back? Was it the depression, the shame of my past, or maybe just plain embarrassment?*

"What brought you back?" she asks.

"Oh, that's a long story. I don't think I can get into it all now, but I got a divorce and needed to be closer to family," I say, my voice trying to sound casual.

"Carly mentioned something about a divorce. I'm really sorry," she says, her sincerity piercing through the small talk.

"It's okay," I say, and for the first time, *I mean it*. "It really is for the best." I'm starting to like my life now—something I haven't been able to say in a long time. I wouldn't want to still be together. This moment of clarity feels strange, but good.

"Jack's boss is going through a divorce, and it's been devastating—even for us on the outside," she says.

"Oh yes, the ripple effects are crazy. My friend Remy probably has second-degree trauma from it," I say, half-joking but knowing there's some truth to it.

"Was it anything in particular, or just a culmination of things?" she asks, gently probing.

"A culmination, I think, with the specific impact of alcohol during the pandemic. If that hadn't happened, we'd probably still be together," I say, but as the words leave my mouth, I know they're not true anymore. I'm relieved we're not. This is a shift—a small but significant one.

"Man, the pandemic really did a number on everyone," she says, shaking her head.

"That's for sure," I reply, feeling the conversation teetering on the edge of something too heavy.

"I'm really sorry. I can only imagine how hard that was," she says, her eyes turning red and teary with genuine empathy.

"It was pretty awful, but thank you. The good thing is that I'm safe, and I'm here, reunited with you," I say, meaning it deeply but ready to move on to lighter topics.

Carly leads us into the conference room, where I'm greeted by the sight of chips, dip, banana bread, an array of sparkling water, and a decadent dessert spread. On the long table, several round wooden embroidery kits are laid out, along with needles, threads in every color, books filled with patterns, and even a light-up board for tracing designs onto fabric.

"Wow, this is incredible," I say, genuinely awed by Carly's ability to pull this off while juggling four kids and a private practice. It's inspiring.

We gather around the table and begin stitching, the conversation flowing effortlessly from politics and the upcoming election to dating and being therapists. We laugh, we share our experiences in therapy, and we wonder how our clients perceive us. By the time the night ends, I feel full—intellectually, emotionally, spiritually.

We walk out to our cars, the warm Ohio wind brushing through my hair. I roll down the window on the drive home, soaking in the gratitude. I've been invited to an annual camping trip with Jude and some other families. I feel included, wanted. Maybe I've finally found my people, and maybe this is exactly where I need to be.

For now, I just want to stay present in this moment—not worry about dating or comparing my life to theirs. I'm happy to be who I am at this stage of life, rebuilding into something beautiful.

8/8/24

FREEDOM

> *"Beware; for I am fearless, and therefore powerful."* ~ Mary Shelley

The next morning, 8/8/2024, I get a text from Tripp: "Divorce decree sent." Three simple words. A weight lifted. I set the phone down, look out my window, and say, "Thank you," to the Universe.

Tripp has finally—*finally*—submitted the divorce decree to the insurance company. Today, I am officially free.

Not when I moved to Ohio.

Not when the divorce was finalized.

Today.

On the Lion's Gate Portal.

For those unfamiliar, the Lion's Gate Portal is an annual astrological event on 8/8—a cosmic reset button for shedding the old and stepping into the new. It's a time of reinvention. Whitney said it best: *"I'm every woman, it's all in meeeeeeeee..."*

I inhale deeply, letting it sink in—*freedom isn't just a legal status. It's an exhale. A heartbeat. A state of being.* I know I won't be truly free if I keep myself tethered to anything—especially something as ridiculous as insurance. I'll deal with the consequences, whatever they may be. My mental and physical freedom is worth more than any bill I'll have to pay. Yes, I'm thousands of dollars in debt, but I have what really matters. I have Jude. I can keep him safe, make the best decisions for him, and sleep at night knowing I did right by him. And I did right by me, too, and that's worth more than any number in my bank account.

"Thank you," I whisper. "Thank you for guiding and protecting me."

I lay back on my bed, smiling, a bubbling excitement growing inside me. "I'm finally free," I say out loud to myself. Then I sit up, as if the realization has struck me for the first time. "I'm finally free!"

I leap to my feet, heart racing, and in one swift motion, I lift open the heavy old window, shove the screen aside, and climb out onto the little roof outside. The shingles are rough under my bare feet, the air cooler than I expected, but I don't care. I feel alive, more alive than I have in years.

And then, at the top of my lungs, I yell, "I'm finally FREEEEEEE!"

The sound echoes into the morning, carrying my joy into the Universe. A neighbor's dog barks back, as if in solidarity, and I laugh so hard I almost lose my balance, grabbing the window frame just in time. But I'm not done. No, I need more.

I stretch my arms out wide, feeling the breeze whip around me, tousling my hair, and I yell again, louder this time, "I'M FUCKIN FREEEEEE!"

Somewhere down the street, I hear a car honk—maybe an irritated driver, or maybe someone cheering me on. I choose to believe the latter. The sun peeks out from behind a cloud, warming my face, and I close my eyes, letting it soak in, feeling like I'm absorbing the Universe's applause.

I start to dance—yes, dance—on that little roof, my feet sliding against the shingles, kicking twigs and bird seed off the roof as I do it. I don't care if I look ridiculous.

"FREEEEEE!" I shout again, throwing my head back to laugh at the sky. The moment is wild, absurd, perfect.

And then, because I'm still me, a tiny thought creeps in: *What if someone sees me? What if I'm not as alone out here as I think I am?* But I push it away, because this is my moment. I don't care if the whole world sees. Let them see. Let them hear. I am free, and I want the Universe to know it.

Finally, too dizzy to stand or dance, I collapse onto the roof, staring up at the endless blue sky. My cheeks ache from smiling, and all I can think is, *This*. This is what it feels like to be truly, completely free.

As I lie here, feeling the rough shingles beneath me and the wide sky above, I raise both my middle fingers toward the heavens, a defiant gesture of victory and release. I hold them there for a moment, grinning like a fool, knowing that the past has nothing on me anymore. Then, slowly, I lower my arms, letting them fall beside me as I sink deeper into the roof, feeling something shift deep inside. It's like the last thread that tied me to the past has finally snapped, and I am floating, untethered, ready for whatever comes next.

Epilogue

12/15/2024

*L*ying awake beneath the cold full moon, the last before the New Year, I'm struck by how time moves so mercilessly forward, leaving fragments of itself behind. A whole year in Ohio—a whole year since I started over—and yet, here I am, in the same bed, beneath the same moon, with a heart that feels completely new.

Jude is nestled against me, his little chest rising and falling in a rhythm that feels older than time. Reese, my loyal Aussie, snores at the foot of the bed, oblivious to the weight of my thoughts. Their small, steady lives ground me. Once, I might have seen this moment as mundane. Now, I understand it as sacred. These breaths, this warmth, this ordinary magic—they are proof that I've survived. That we've survived.

The world outside our little cocoon? It's as unpredictable as ever —or maybe it isn't. Women are still losing elections to the same man, his chaos eclipsing their competence. A handsome Ivy League graduate murders a health insurance CEO, sparking celebration in the streets of NYC and exposing the simmering resentment toward an industry complicit in harm. Over in New Jersey, the skies are alive with drones or UFOs. People say the aliens are visiting, but I wonder if they're leaving. If even they've had enough. The government has finally admitted they exist, many believed to be lurking in the deep oceans. Somehow, that feels fitting. The mysteries of the Universe hidden in the depths of dark waters, only to emerge when everything feels upside down.

It's been over a year since Tripp saw Jude. That truth clings to me, painful and complicated. There's sadness, yes—because how could there not be? But there's also quiet relief. *Addiction is a thief*, stealing in ways that don't always make sense. I've learned to stop mourning what was never mine to fix. Maybe that's the real change: *I've stopped being the heroine in someone else's tragedy.* I've started trusting the messy, unknowable process of life. Trusting that no matter what, Jude and I will be okay. Not because the world is predictable or fair, but because we are resilient. Because we've had to be.

Before I shut my eyes, I begin a ritual for the full moon, one I found on none other than TikTok. The idea is that the full moon is a perfect time to illuminate our shadow self—the thoughts or behaviors that don't align with who I want to be. So, I begin to write. It feels silly at first—how could lighting a candle and writing things down change anything? But when I close my eyes, the answer is obvious. It's not about changing the world; it's about changing the way I carry it. So, I let go of the blame I've been holding onto. The stories I've told myself about what I should have done, what I should have seen. How absurd it is to expect myself to be a fortune teller. To believe that not foreseeing every disaster is some kind of moral failing. The world doesn't work like that. Life doesn't work like that. I've learned that I can lose everything I thought I needed and still find myself whole. That's my superpower. Give me the worst, and I'll show you my best.

With this sentiment, a quiet excitement stirs inside me. It feels like New Year's Eve is already here. There's no need for glittering mirror balls or champagne-soaked resolutions because this feeling is quieter, more sacred. This moment isn't for promises to the future; it's for honoring the wins I've already earned. No one else may see them, but I do. I feel them in the lightness of my chest, in the way my breath doesn't catch when I think of the past anymore. I feel them in Jude's laughter and Reese's snores, in the soft glow of the moon casting shadows that no longer scare me. I may not know where this current is taking me, but for the first time, I'm letting it carry me. I trust it to.

So tonight, under the cold full moon, I'm saying thank you. For the heartbreak and the healing. For the chaos and the clarity. For the losses that taught me to hold on and the wins that taught me to let go. Thank you—for nothing...and everything.

Acknowledgments

Writing this book has been equal parts soul excavation and life restoration, and it wouldn't have been possible without the people who supported me.

First, to **Usher Morgan**, thank you for recognizing the value of this story and believing it was one the world needed to hear. Your faith in this book—and in me—has meant more than I can possibly express. Thank you for making this dream a reality.

To **Katie Vincent**, my editor and magician, thank you for turning my tense issues (and emotional ones) into something coherent. You're a truly special soul, and I'm endlessly grateful for you.

To my **coven of women**: whether you were listed in these pages or remained the steady hum of support in the background, thank you. You howled at the moon with me, held me when I felt like breaking, and reminded me that survival is both a solo and a team sport. Your strength is woven into every word of this book.

To the **Mend with Mere community**—the workshop attendees, the channel supporters, and all the incredible souls who have embraced my work—thank you. Your encouragement and unwavering support have meant the world to me.

To those I unintentionally neglected during my grief—friends and family I couldn't support in the ways you deserved—I see you, I love you, and I'm deeply sorry. Thank you for understanding that I was in survival mode.

To my family: **Mom, Dad, Leslie, Keagan, and Bella**—thank you for being my safety net and my constant reminders that love doesn't have to be perfect to be unconditional. You've carried me through this chapter. I love you.

To my son, you are the brightest light in my life: thank you for choosing me to be your mom. I love you.

To my spirit guides and ancestors, thank you for being my unseen safety net. I will proudly run with the baton you passed to me, carrying your wisdom, love, and guidance as I move forward—honoring all that you've given and all that you've endured.

Finally, to anyone who picks up this book and allows these words into their life—thank you. I am profoundly grateful to share this journey with you, and I hope it speaks to the fire within you, stoking its strength and brilliance as you move forward.